The Evergreen Community:

CREATIVE TEACHING IDEAS FROM *EVERGREEN* CLASSROOMS

to accompany
Evergreen: A Guide to Writing
Fifth Edition
and
Evergreen with Readings: A Guide to Writing
Fifth Edition

Susan Fawcett

Alvin Sandberg

HOUGHTON MIFFLIN COMPANY   BOSTON   TORONTO
St. Charles, Illinois   Palo Alto   Princeton, New Jersey

Sponsoring Editor: Renée Deljon
Senior Associate Editor: Ellen Darion
Development Editor: Melody Davies
Senior Project Editor: Rosemary Winfield
Editorial Assistant: Gabrielle Stone
Senior Manufacturing Coordinator: Priscilla Bailey
Marketing Manager: Pamela Laskey
Editorial Intern: Eliza Patten

Printed in the U.S.A.

ISBN: 0-395-75036-9

123456789–VG–00 99 98 97 96

Contents

From the President of
the National Association
of Developmental Educators

Dear Colleagues:

I welcome the opportunity to write in support of *The Evergreen Community*, the new teaching resource for the tried and true *Evergreen* and *Evergreen with Readings*. Over the span of my career, I have either adopted or personally developed teaching techniques that consistently work for me and my students, and I continue to use these techniques successfully. Like all dedicated professionals, however, I am always on the lookout for fresh teaching ideas to employ in the classroom. Some I pick up from seminars, workshops, conferences, and informal discussions; others I glean from articles in professional publications—an idea here, an idea there. Yet rarely do I hit the bonanza of a resource like *The Evergreen Community*.

Because developmental educators are first and foremost teachers, and *The Evergreen Community* is a teacher's book, I find it an exciting and important contribution to our rapidly growing field. As a developmental educator, my commitments have been first to my students and second to the development of my profession; this publication offers a wealth of suggestions, approaches, and activities that will prove invaluable to both. Through this resource, developmental education practitioners can share the experience and creativity of their peers, benefiting from their numerous and diverse contributions.

I commend those who saw the need for such a publication and made it happen. *The Evergreen Community* befits the people whom I most respect and admire: the dedicated professionals in my field of developmental education and the aspiring students they serve so well.

Gene Beckett

Gene Beckett
Shawnee State University
President, National Association of Developmental Educators

Welcome to
The Evergreen Community

Welcome to the First Edition of *The Evergreen Community*. Whether you have been teaching with *Evergreen* since its beginnings or are new to it this term, you will find here a wealth of classroom-inspired and class-tested teaching ideas, all contributed by the users of *Evergreen* and *Evergreen with Readings*.

The community of instructors and students using *Evergreen* has been growing steadily for twenty years, and this collection of teaching tips and techniques marks our commitment to bringing the community and its resources together. It is, most simply, our response to instructors' frequent requests for new teaching ideas. Now, by simply paging through *The Evergreen Community*, you can find fresh activities, assignments, and strategies for using journals, teaching argument, and motivating students.

I want to thank our contributors to date and urge all *Evergreen* instructors to send us new *Evergreen* teaching tips. Also, please let your students know that we invite them to send us their comments, whether on *Evergreen*, their experience as learners, writing, English classes in general—it's up to them. Our fundamental goal is to build a large and varied *Evergreen Community*, one that helps you help students to learn—and that enhances your own pleasure and success as an educator. Enjoy!

Renée Deljon
Sponsoring Editor
Developmental English

Renee_Deljon@hmco.com

1

Creating a Writers' Community

The great strength of *Evergreen* is that everything about it is high-quality, reflecting sincere awareness of and concern with the students and the learning process.

Betty Owen, Broward County Community College, FL

I predict that *Evergreen* will always be very high on the list of texts considered for our developmental composition course. The readings are an attractive supplement. Throughout, you present instruction, examples, and models written in an unbiased, nonsexist, and encouraging style.
You really do have a winner in this textbook—hard to beat!

Linda Whisnant, Guilford Technical Community College, NC

Establishing a Learner-Friendly Atmosphere

My students know from achievement test scores and from their own experience in English classes that they need to improve their writing, grammar, and communication skills. Many are frightened at being in an English class and have a valid dislike for anything at all that has to do with an English class.

From the first moment we meet, I try to establish a comfortable, relaxed, safe, positive, equitable atmosphere. I explain the goals and objectives in the course curriculum and describe how we will work to complete and achieve them. My students know exactly what is expected and how we are going to achieve that together. I continue to maintain this atmosphere throughout the semester; therefore, I have an excellent response from my students. When they realize they are in a nonthreatening environment, they feel free to be themselves, and they become creative and productive.

As a motivational technique, I read aloud essays written by former students, from the most recent classes I have taught. I pass each of the essays around after reading it, and we discuss it in specific detail in order to grasp why it is well written. I present an overview of the essay and dissect each stage of development in easy, simplistic terms. My classes thereby get to hear the sound of a good essay, see the format, and view in detail each example offered. I try to demystify the procedure and process for them; I even tell them this is show and tell. They laugh. I state that writing is a skill like any other and that we get better at it by practicing. I explain that I work to improve my writing and communication skills all the time. My students know I expect to receive essays of at least five paragraphs, and because I have this expectation, they rise to the occasion, expect more of themselves, and produce. Using this philosophy, attitude, and technique with my classes has always had positive results: outstanding essays.

From Jane Wilson, Ivy Technical State College, IN

Class Project: Team Writing Exercise

We discuss Chapters 5–12 (developing the different kinds of paragraphs) early in the semester. At this point in the term, students are still not entirely comfortable with the class, their own writing skills, or their classmates. The intriguing picture at the end of Chapter 6, "Narration" (see p. 84) helps me alleviate some of these discomforts.

The class is divided into groups of five or six students. We first discuss how to write narration, and we spend some time asking questions about the picture and its characters. Each group is then asked to write a short story about the picture—one story per group, one grade per group.

Students who are shy about participating in a class brainstorming session find it much easier to respond in a small group. Ideas may come slowly at first, but they soon flow freely (and sometimes hilariously). Most students get caught up in the enthusiasm of the situation.

The next step in the group's writing process is deciding which ideas to use and which to discard—a useful skill for a writer. In this part of the process, the students are learning the art of compromise and are developing teamwork skills.

At this point, one student is assigned to put the story on paper as the group dictates. Once the initial effort is on paper, the editing process begins. Many times peer or group editing efforts fall short of the goal because students have difficulty with constructive, honest criticism. (It is so easy to say to another student, "This sounds all right to me.") With a common grade hanging in the balance, however, the participants are more likely to point out errors or concerns. When there is disagreement, some of the groups actually consult the text for help.

The stories I receive are extremely entertaining and imaginative; however, the real benefits of the project go far beyond the stories themselves. By the time we have completed this exercise, the students have lost (or at least reduced) their fear of exposing their ideas and skills to the scrutiny of their classmates. They have learned to look up answers to their own questions, and they may have gained some knowledge about grammar and mechanics and the writing process.

I have found this assignment to be a definite "win-win" situation!

From Suzanne Doonan, Pennsylvania Institute of Technology, PA

The Biography Poem

The biography poem has been a successful activity that I've used to enhance students' self-esteem and to provide a publishing opportunity. It works best with a small, cohesive, trusting group. I introduce the activity by modeling the writing process. Depicting the class group as having a distinctive personality, I solicit descriptions of class traits and a name for the group. I demonstrate writing, revising, and editing the poem on the chalkboard. Then students write their own biography poems for a class publication.

Chatterboxes

Funny, sarcastic, truthful, sincere
Students of Mrs. Doonan
Lovers of learning and people
Who feel blessed and determined
Who fear rejection and failing
Who would like to come out on top
Friends

From Patricia Malinowski, Finger Lakes Community College, NY

The Group Chapter

The group chapter—a chapter that I work through with the entire class—allows the instructor to designate a time for whole-class discussion or collaborative work on specific topics. Suggested topics:

Unit	*Evergreen* Chapters	Topics
I	1, 2,	Prewriting
	3	Rudiments of the Paragraph
II	4	Paragraph unity
	17, 19	Mini-essay
III	17	Parts of the essay

The above-suggested chapters can be assigned so that students will be prepared for class discussion to be held at least once a week.

Peer Editing

The use of peer editing derives from an understanding of revision as the process of "seeing again." When students share their ideas, they begin to see that their writing does have worth. Second, they become more aware of audience and purpose. Finally, if approached in a positive manner, students readily offer constructive criticism to their peers, as well as support. Several methods of peer editing have been tried:

1. As a group, students are asked to draw up a list of positive comments to make about their peers' writing. They use the list to comment on one another's work and are then encouraged to put their comments in writing.

2. The instructor distributes a list of questions for students to answer about a writing assignment. Here are some examples: What is this paper about? What has the author stated well? Do you want more information about a particular incident? Can you suggest other examples, support, or evidence that the author might include? Students exchange papers and answer the questions in writing. Papers are returned to the original owners for revision.

3. Student papers are collected, names are removed, and the papers are redistributed randomly. Peer editors then map the papers. Both the original paper and the map are returned to the author. The author has the opportunity to add information on the basis of any gaps in the map.

Additional information about peer editing is available in *Beat Not the Poor Desk* by Marie Ponsot and Rosemary Deen (Boynton/Cook Publishers, Inc., 1982).

From William G. Thomas, Los Angeles Trade Technical College, CA

Creating Community in the Classroom

I begin the term referring both to the beginning and the middle of the text. This weaves together the "concepts" of paragraph building and the rhetorical approaches to writing, grammar, spelling, punctuation, and other mechanics. The author selections are used for critical reading, and students respond to questions suggested as well as to others that may be relevant. Many of my students, since we are primarily an inner-city, vocationally oriented college, are foreign-born or have had a "Swiss cheese" education in English. Accordingly, reading with comprehension is new, and important, to most of them.

The drills are completed as part of the weekly homework, along with one or more written assignments each week. I use "learning groups" or "teams," much like a writers' workshop, so students assist one another and interact a great deal. Our weekly routine, for our three one-hour sessions, includes: day one—first draft, which the team members review with one another while I serve as a consultant; day two—second draft, where students discuss their respective improvement techniques; and day three—the selection by each group of their "best" paper, which, if time and other class commitments allow, is read by a representative student from the group. The class as a whole votes on the best paper, but students are not allowed to ballot for their own teams' papers. I reward winners with candy bars, pens—whatever inexpensive items I can find as bribery.

For the drills, which we use on a daily basis, drawn directly from *Evergreen,* the teams, usually six in number, complete in turn and receive plus or minus points for their answers. Every few weeks, I add up the scores and once more play the bribery game.

Intermittently, and at the end of the semester, I check each student's *Evergreen* to ensure that *all* assignments have been completed. I insist that if they expect me to be prepared to teach, they must be prepared to learn.

At the last class meeting, prior to the final examination, the students evaluate the class with "no holds bared." Our objective is to collectively suggest improvements from which future classes will benefit. *Evergreen* consistently draws raves and for all the right reasons.

From the above, you can readily imagine why I plan to continue the use of this fine developmental English text, as well as to use its garden-titled (Grassroots) companion in other developmental classes.

From William G. Thomas, Los Angeles Trade Technical College, CA

Cross-Cultural Community

As a term paper in my developmental English class (which uses *Evergreen*), I require the preparation of a cross-cultural paper by each student. The topic can be any aspect, characteristic, feature, or person (or whatever) of a culture other than one's own. We also eliminate the U.S.A. because we're already in that culture. Thus, a twenty-year-old from El Salvador, majoring in nursing, might write about childbirth practices in India. A Los Angeles native could choose education in Costa Rica; a Mexican-American, chastity in Ethiopia—the subjects have been endless.

The process is uncomplicated. After almost three-quarters of the semester has passed, students feel quite comfortable with the classroom environment, with one another, and with me (if they still laugh at all my jokes). For up to six class sessions, students from a particular area of the globe—Asia, Central America, the Caribbean, South America, Africa, and Europe—serve as a panel (much like "Meet the Press"). They tell their classmates a bit about their native countries and why they came to the United States, and provide examples of common and different cultural practices and major historical events.

Recently, we had a Caribbean panel with one fortyish student who had spent four years in a Cuban prison, and the Asian panel included an older student who, as a South Vietnamese army lieutenant, was captured by the enemy and spent seven years in a prison camp. The world of the past confronted all of us in the realities and personal experiences that were shared.

From Karen O'Donnell, Finger Lakes Community College, NY

Cooperative Learning Activity

First, I have to introduce to my students the concept of group roles, those of recorder, observer, encourager, researcher, and checker. The recorder takes notes and is the record keeper. The observer watches how well the groups works together and notices whether all group members are participating. The encourager helps draw other students out by saying such things as "What do you think?" or "Tell us more" or "What is your idea?" The researcher looks up information for the group when necessary and gets and returns supplies. The checker makes sure everyone understands, keeps everyone on task, and seeks help if necessary. I give all students a handout explaining all the roles, give role cards to each group during cooperative activities, and randomly assign roles and switch roles for other activities.

To actually teach prewriting, I use cooperative groups. First, I divide the class into groups of three, four, or five members, using some random basis; this depends on class size. The ideal is four to a group. This will form base groups. Next, I have the groups count off (1, 2, 3, 4; 1, 2, and so on), then I have the ones group together, the twos group together, and so on, to form the expert groups. Each expert group will be assigned to learn one of the first four types of prewriting activities in Chapter 2 of the text *Evergreen* by Fawcett and Sandberg: freewriting, brainstorming, clustering, and asking questions. Each expert group will develop the topic "College" (or any other chosen topic), using their individual method of prewriting so that they can bring an example back to their base groups. I randomly assign roles to each member of the expert group.

When the expert groups are finished, each member, returning to his or her base group, teaches the prewriting activity just learned. (I also randomly assign roles in the base groups.) Then the base groups develop another topic, such as "Writing," using all four of the prewriting skills, and the results are hung on the walls of the classroom. I find this technique very effective because there can be transfer from short-term to long-term memory through the use of rehearsal and recoding.

2
Assessing Student Writing

The greatest strength of *Evergreen* is its comprehensive coverage of writing skills, its excellent reading selections and examples, and its use of "stand alone" chapters that permit instructors to organize instruction as best suits their needs.

Meredith A. Wilson, Solano Community College, CA

. . . the effective content in each section of *Evergreen* has allowed me to use one text instead of three for instruction on the writing process, grammar and sentence structure, and summary writing based on readings.

Margaret Koenig, Monterey Peninsula College, CA

From Patricia Malinowski, Finger Lakes Community College, NY

Diagnosis

The first step in teaching the College Composition course is to assess the writing abilities of each student. At a community college, our population is drawn from a multitude of educational backgrounds. The students who have enrolled in this course have been advised to do so on the basis of their scores on the reading placement test (Descriptive Test of Language Skills [DTLS], published by the College Board), a writing sample (evaluated by a member of the Humanities Department and the Developmental Studies Department), or prior academic record. Because of this diversity, it is important to establish the skill level of each student at the beginning of the semester. Once this assessment has been made, the instructor can best facilitate the student's individual growth.

It is suggested that on the first day of class, after briefly explaining the College Composition course to the students and distributing course outlines and requirements, the instructor can have students take one, two, or all three of the diagnostic tests on pages 12–13. Judging from instructors' past experience, two diagnostic paragraphs is an adequate sample. Follow up with the Diagnostic Survey on page 14.

Once the student has completed this process, the instructor should be able to assess the student's capabilities, both in the framework of holistic writing and in regard to specific grammar problems. From this assessment comes the assignment of individual grammar chapters in the *Evergreen* text.

Sample Diagnostic Paragraphs

Diagnostic Paragraph I

Write an essay about one of the following topics. Hand in all your work. Simply underline any words that you do not know how to spell.

1. Give your impressions of a recent concert you attended: the crowd, the performers, or the music.

2. Is television harmful or not? Use specific examples.

3. Describe a law you believe is unfair and explain your view.

4. What changes would you make at your job, at school, or in your family?

5. What movie, book, television program, or concert has made a strong impression on you, and why?

Alternate Diagnostic Paragraph I

Write a paragraph about ONE of the following topics. Hand in all your work. Simply underline any words that you do not know how to spell.

1. People do various things to relax. Describe what you do to relax and explain why you think it is the best method of relaxation.

2. We have all met, at some time, an unusual person. Describe such a person and explain why that person is unique.

3. Describe a place you like to visit and offer reasons why someone else would enjoy visiting that place.

Diagnostic Writing II

Over the past several years, different government commissions and independent research organizations have found that the American educational system is declining. Different groups have cited various reasons for this decline.

Read the article on the back of this page.* Use your own experiences to either agree or disagree with the author's thesis regarding education and the direction of education in America.

Use the space below for outlining or organizing your ideas.

Diagnostic Paragraph III

Interview one of your classmates.

Using the information you have obtained in your interview, write a paragraph in which you introduce your classmate to the entire class.

---

*Stanley Thompson, "Students Responsible for Failure to Learn," *Los Angeles Times.*

Diagnostic Survey

Answer each of the following questions.

1. How do you feel about writing?

2. Why do you feel this way?

3. What are your strengths and weaknesses in writing?

4. What have you done to strengthen and improve your writing skills?

5. List any college writing or English courses you have taken.

6. Additional comments:

From Patricia Malinowski, Finger Lakes Community College, NY

College Composition Writing Outcomes

Writing is a process, and below are means of measuring students' outcomes.

Unit I: The student

- Indicates mastery of the paragraph:
    develops one idea well
    uses a topic sentence
    has appropriate supporting details
    can "close" ideas

- Can use simple sentences; indicates ability to use compound sentences.

- Can begin to use rhetorical patterns of description and narration.

- Makes grammatical errors, but they do not interfere with the expression of ideas.

- Makes spelling errors; indicates ability to identify them.

Unit II: The student

- Indicates mastery of the mini-essay:
    all points under mastery of the paragraph; can also write adequate introductory, body, and concluding paragraphs

- Can use simple and compound sentences; indicates use of complex sentences.

- Can use several rhetorical patterns.

- Is starting to identify grammar problems independently and correct them.

- Indicates ability to correct spelling errors.

Unit III: The student

- Indicates mastery of multiple-paragraph essay; can develop a thesis and give it adequate support.

- Can use transitional words and phrases, a variety of sentence patterns, and several rhetorical modes.

- Makes fewer grammatical errors; has ability to correct errors and work through multiple revisions.

- Shows an increased confidence in writing abilities.

Conference Component

One important component in this course is the Conference Component.

It is advisable for the instructor to try to set time aside each week, during class sessions or during office hours, to meet with individual students regarding their progress in the course. The instructor should be prepared to discuss and to answer questions about those students' writing and grammar assignments.

It is especially advisable for the instructor to continually relay to the student what progress is being made, as well as updates as to where the student is with regard to course requirements. Use of the writing outcomes is extremely helpful in assessing student progress. These outcomes should be shared with students at the beginning of the semester.

COLLEGE COMPOSITION
Evaluation Sheet

Sentence Structure

    Subject/verb   _____

    Fragments   _____

    Run-ons   _____

Paragraphing

    Topic sentence   _____

    Support   _____

    Transitional phrases   _____

    Organization

        Time order   _____

        Space order   _____

        Order of importance   _____

Mini-Essay

    Introduction   _____

    Middle paragraph(s)   _____

    Conclusion   _____

Essay

    Introduction

        Effective opening   _____

        Thesis statement   _____

        Preview   _____

    Middle paragraphs

        Topic sentences   _____

        Support   _____

    Conclusion   _____

Punctuation

    Commas   _____

    Periods   _____

    Apostrophes   _____

    Quotations   _____

Spelling   _____

Parts of Speech

    Subject/verb agreement   _____

    Plurals   _____

    Pronoun agreement   _____

    Verb tense   _____

    Adjectives/adverbs   _____

COLLEGE COMPOSITION
Alternate Evaluation Sheet

Sentence Structure

    Subject/verb   _____

    Fragments   _____

    Run-ons   _____

Paragraphing

    Topic sentence   _____

    Support   _____

    Transitional phrases   _____

    Organization

        Time order   _____

        Space order   _____

        Order of importance   _____

Paragraph Types

    Description   _____

    Illustration   _____

    Comparison/contrast   _____

    Process   _____

    Persuasion   _____

Punctuation

    Commas   _____

    Periods   _____

    Apostrophes   _____

    Quotations   _____

Spelling   _____

Parts of Speech

    Subject/verb agreement   _____

    Plurals   _____

    Pronoun agreement   _____

    Verb tense   _____

    Adjectives/adverbs   _____

Dictionary Skills   _____

The BSA 025 Writing Portfolio

The BSA 025 writing portfolio is a collection of the semester's writing accomplishments. It gives you a forum in which to demonstrate your mastery of various writing techniques. The portfolio is an important part of your course grade (50%). This portfolio will provide an overview of your growth and development as a writer.

The BSA 025 writing portfolio must include *revised* copies of two, of the three essays assigned during the semester—introduction, information, persuasion. These copies must be typed or word-processed. The draft copies of these essays, with instructor comments and corrections, must also be included. The portfolio must contain four of your in-class writings, with instructor comments. (Although the choice of which writings to include is yours, the final in-class assignment from session #28 must be one of the writings included.) In addition, the research paper, as originally submitted, must also appear in your portfolio. The collection of writings must be introduced by a cover memo.

- The BSA 025 writing portfolio is to be placed in a 3-prong *pocket* folder.
- All portfolios are due as indicated in your syllabus—session #30. *No late portfolios will be accepted! There are no exceptions to this rule!*

Cover Memo

The cover memo is your opportunity to evaluate your writing experience. You might, for example, discuss what writing strategies and techniques you have learned, what writing weaknesses you have overcome, what weaknesses you have yet to overcome, or what strengths you have discovered in your writing. This memo is an important part of your portfolio and should be crafted with great care.

BSA 025 WRITING PORTFOLIO CHECKLIST

Place a check by each item as it is completed and inserted into the portfolio. Please place the items in the order given.

_____ 1. Three-prong pocket folder

_____ 2. Portfolio checklist (to be placed in front pocket of folder)

_____ 3. Cover memo

_____ 4. First revised essay (introduction, information, or persuasion)

_____ 5. Draft copy of this essay (with instructor comments)

_____ 6. Second revised essay

_____ 7. Draft copy of this essay (with instructor comments)

_____ 8. Three in-class writings (unrevised, with instructor comments)

_____ 9. Final in-class writing (to be placed in back pocket of folder)

_____ 10. Research paper (to be placed in back pocket of folder)

— **Important** —
If you do not submit a writing portfolio, you will fail BSA 025!

_____
(student signature)

_____
(date)

3

Incorporating the Writing Process

The expanded coverage of journal writing is very good. I like the prompts *Evergreen* provides. It helps students discover themselves and their ideas, and they are more apt to do that if they feel that the journal writing doesn't have to be "ready for a grade."

Linda Whisnant, Guilford Technical Community College, NC

The journal coverage is excellent. Journal writing is important at the developmental level, and the additional information is well done.

Debra Anderson, Indian River Community College, FL

From Susan R. McKnight, Tarrant County Junior College, TX

Promoting Student-Text Interaction

Whenever my developmental English students complete a reading assignment, they write one page in a double-entry journal. This learning tool helps them think about what they have read, relate to it personally, and reflect on how the material fits into the context of the whole course. While I use this exercise in English classes, it is a writing-across-the-curriculum strategy useful in any discipline.

The two parts of the journal are "What's It About?" and "What Does It Mean to Me?" Students may establish their own format. Some like to use the top half of the page for "What's it about?", in which they state three or four specific facts they consider most important in that reading. Below it, in the "What does it mean to me?" section, they can respond in a number of ways to show evidence of critical thinking about the material. For example, they may choose to respond to questions such as these: How do I agree or disagree with the author's ideas? How can I apply what I learned to a new situation? If a problem is posed, are the solutions sensible? What new ideas occurred to me as I read? Another possible format, the side-by-side arrangement, allows students to respond directly to each of the main points of the lesson.

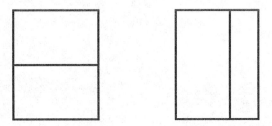

In addition to encouraging interaction with the text and critical thinking, the journals are an excellent tool for beginning class. I may start a discussion by simply requesting, "Take out your journals and tell us one significant point you gained from your reading for today." I know that even the most reluctant student has something to say, and that he or she knows that at this point, any answer is correct because the response is whatever the student deems important, not a guess-what-the-instructor-has-in-mind answer.

Of course this academic journal can be modified to fit a specific assignment. Students can use it for short in-class writing assignments or add answers to the daily entry for a quiz. Sometimes I specifically request that "What does it mean to me?" be completed in class, so that they can have some additional time between the reading and the rethinking. Since I often check journal entries during the first ten minutes of class, writing them encourages promptness as well as completeness. The original thinking reflected in them often serves as a starting point for writing essays. At the end of the semester, another advantage is that the completed journal is an excellent tool for reviewing the course.

This type of journal works very well with the readings in our *Evergreen* text. For instance, when I introduced the reading "How to Get the Most Out of Yourself" by Alan Loy McGinnis, I asked the students to read only the first three paragraphs, McGinnis's introduction linking self-image and success, and to write in their journals at least two ideas that caught their attention and a personal comment about each. Before I assigned the rest of the reading for homework, we took time to hear several of these initial journal entries. My goal at this point was simply to engage the students' interest in the topic of the article and have them anticipate the direction McGinnis's advice would take. Their assignment after reading the article was to complete a double entry in their journals for Discussion and Writing Questions 1 and 2. In the following class their journal comments began our discussion and served as a transition to a subsequent writing assignment, a choice from Writing Assignments (1–3).

Initially students may question the value of the journal, but generally after a few weeks they realize they are retaining more information and thinking about it in a new way. This assignment should never become humdrum. The number of ways the double-entry journal can be varied is limited only by the instructor's imagination.

From Keysha Ingram-Gamor, Montgomery College, MD

Emotional Scavenger Hunt

Students are to keep a journal for one week prior to the "Description" chapter. They should write about things that they experience during the course of the day, as in a diary. Students are told that they will use the material somehow the following week, but they are not given any more specific details or instructions. At some point during the chapter on description, students are instructed to go through this journal, searching for all their expressions of emotions, jotting them down as they progress through their record of the week. Whatever emotion is dominant will be the one they will use for their writing assignment. Now it's time to describe the abstract emotion that is dominant in their journal. Students share this emotion with the class, under the constraint of not using the actual word (or synonyms or antonyms for this emotion). The class will guess the emotion by listening to each description. This activity can be used competitively for an inexpensive prize, such as a can of a beverage or a vending machine snack or a piece of fruit. Students can simply use an ordinary sheet of paper for their scoring sheet. The teacher will be the host, reading each description, and the students will be the contestants.

From June J. McManus, San Antonio College, TX

Journal Assignments

When I assign a reading from *Evergreen* to be read before students come to class, they may choose to relate to it in some way in their journals immediately after reading. Then, at the beginning of class, I almost always assign a ten-minute journal entry relating to the reading. For example, when they read Richard Rodriquez, I may ask them to write about an experience they had on a summer job, or when I assign Martin Luther King, I may ask them to write about the absence or presence of racism on our campus.

Journal Assignment for English 301

Purpose of the Journal

To make the student more comfortable with writing, through using what he or she is learning or has learned or experienced as sources for creative thinking and essay writing.

Requirements

An 8½ × 11" lightweight looseleaf notebook; title page with name, course, section. Minimum of five entries a week, dated. Circle the dates of two each week for me to read. Writing every day is beneficial. Varied entries, in-class writing and out-of-class writing. Students should bring journals to class every day.

Instructions

- Begin with a title page
- Write for yourself. You are your audience.
- Write a summary of each assigned essay. Then comment in some way on the essay.
- You may write about any experience outside this class—television shows, newspaper articles, cartoons, movies, other classes.
- You will freewrite at the beginning of almost every class period. It is important that you bring your journal to class every day. These in-class entries are required.
- Read your choice of several unassigned essays from your textbook and respond to them. Many essays deal with science, nature, history, or other topics of interest to you. Look at Rhetorical Index for classification of subject matter.

(continued)

Journal Assignment for English 301

Instructions (continued)

- Plan future educational experiences—reading, television, movies, museum visits, symphony concerts.
- Read over your journal occasionally. Comment on conclusions you can draw about yourself or your writing progress.
** • Avoid writing about your love life or personal problems unless they relate to this course.
- Keep a personal spelling list at the end of your journal. Add to it throughout the semester.

Grading

The journal will be taken up twice during the semester and then, finally, near the end of the semester. Each time I take the journal up, will respond to two entries per week, but I will not mark mechanical errors. I will make suggestions and comments. Your final journal will be graded. This grade has the same value as the final exam. See your assignment sheet for due dates.

From Patricia Malinowski, Finger Lakes Community College, NY

Journals

An important part of the College Composition course is encouraging the student to write often and at length. One of the most effective ways to accomplish this goal is through the weekly journal. This journal encourages the students to write both about themselves and about topical issues. It is suggested that the journal entry be of a specific length, such as two handwritten pages (both sides of a single sheet) or one computer-typed page. It is also suggested that journal writing be presented in a nonthreatening manner: that is, that it not be corrected for grammatical errors or graded. The journal can additionally be used to move the student from personal writing (subjective: Journal 1 Autobiography) to academic writing (objective). Some suggested modes for inclusion are summary writing, letters to the editor, and letters of job application. Current research shows that the journal is effective in lowering writing anxiety and motivating students to express themselves freely at length. The journal should also serve as a means of making the instructor better acquainted with the student, and as an unofficial record of the student's growth.

SAMPLES

Journal Assignments Sheet

Journal Topic Sheets (3) A new topic sheet might be distributed at the beginning of each unit.

JOURNAL ASSIGNMENTS

One journal entry (front and back of a sheet of standard notebook paper) is due each week. You should follow the schedule below:

UNIT I

Journal 1   —   Autobiographical
Journal 2   —   Descriptive
Journal 3   —   Topic Sheet Choice
Journal 4   —   Free
Journal 5   —   Topic Sheet Choice

UNIT II

Journal 6   —   Process
Journal 7   —   Topic Sheet Choice
Journal 8   —   Example
Journal 9   —   Free
Journal 10   —   Topic Sheet Choice

UNIT III

Journal 11   —   Topic Sheet Choice
Journal 12   —   Comparison/Contrast
Journal 13   —   Topic Sheet Choice
Journal 14   —   Persuasive
Journal 15   —   Free

For Journals:

1. Due on the day stated on class assignment sheet.

2. Please state at the top of your journal entry the topic you have selected.

3. Also state at the top what skill you are presently working on: for example, Verb Tense

If you are unable to fill the space allotted to the assigned topic, complete the journal entry by writing about any topic you wish. There is no excuse for an incomplete journal entry!

Journal Topic Sheet #1

The journal topics for this unit will be taking a bit of a different direction from your previous assignments. In this unit, we hope to introduce you to some additional basic writing skills that you will use in your college career.

The journal topics for this unit will require more time, but you will be given specific assignments and directions for each. There will also be two assignments that will be completed on the computer.

The rules for journal assignments remain the same: if handwritten, a sheet front and back; if done on the computer, one sheet. Assignments are due on the day specified on the calendar.

The schedule for this unit is as follows:

Journal 11 — Writing a summary
Journal 12 — Comparison and contrast of ideas (computer)
Journal 13 — Using other sources to support your opinion (Persuasion)
Journal 14 — More persuasion (computer)
Journal 15 — Letter writing

It is important that you understand the requirements for each of the assignments. If you are not sure, ASK.

Examples

1. Give examples of pet peeves that you have.
2. Give examples of problems you face at home, school, or work. Explain these examples thoroughly.
3. Give examples of changes you would like to make in a product. You might consider a car, a TV, and so on.

Comparison/Contrast

4. Compare and contrast your parents' and your own attitudes toward some subjects. You might consider work, school, dating, marriage. . . .
5. Compare and contrast how a favorite place looks during two different seasons.
6. Compare and contrast the experience of going out to a movie and watching a movie on TV.

Persuasive

7. Write a memo to your employer persuading him or her to change some aspect of your job, or to give you a raise.
8. Write a letter to a close friend who has asked you for advice on a major decision he or she has to make. You might write about remaining in school, applying for a college internship, changing jobs, and so on.
9. Support or refute the idea that your high school years are the best time of your life.
10. Persuade me to buy a new car, a new vacuum cleaner, a . . . !

Journal Topic Sheet #2

1. Describe career opportunities for your field.
2. Describe some childhood memories. What is your earliest?
3. Describe a local tourist attraction (e.g., a lake, an oceanfront beach, a gorge or mountain, a state park).
4. Describe a pet or other favorite animal.
5. Describe whom and what you would like to take with you on a very long space voyage.

Narrative

6. Describe an incident in which you were treated unfairly or felt cheated.
7. Write your own fantasy or science fiction tale.
8. Relate a humorous incident from your past.

Process

9. Explain one of the processes connected with your job (e.g., creating an ad, food preparation, cashing out customers).
10. Describe a familiar process (e.g., school registration, registering a car, taking a driving test).
11. Explain the steps involved in teaching someone to _____ (e.g., ski, drive, quilt, crochet, weld).

Examples

12. Choose five of your positive qualities and give several examples to support your statement that you have them.
13. Give examples of some unfair laws. Why are they unfair?
14. Give examples that demonstrate that "experience is the best teacher" or that "you can't judge a book by its cover."

Comparison/Contrast

15. Compare and contrast high school and college.
16. Things seem to change as we grow older. Write about the changes in your feelings toward someone or something, from when you were a child to now.
17. Compare and contrast two cities or two vacation spots.
18. Compare and contrast two brands of something (e.g., two makes of cars, two brands of cereal).

Persuasive

19. Persuade me to purchase (or not to purchase) a certain item (e.g., a car, a VCR, a gun).
20. Persuade me to eat (or not to eat) at _____ (e.g., McDonald's Wendy's, Burger King).
21. Should teachers give exams? Write a convincing response.
22. Should spelling and grammar be considered in the scoring of an essay exam in a class other than English? Explain your view in a way that will attract others' support.
23. Should students have to take courses outside of their majors (e.g., English, mathematics, psychology, sociology, speech)?

Journal Topic Sheet #3

Descriptive

1. Describe a trip you have always dreamed of taking. You might consider Hawaii, Australia, and so on.

2. Imagine that you are employed by a nationally famous toymaker. You have been told to design a toy likely to become a national fad, such as the Cabbage Patch Kids. Describe the toy you would design.

3. Describe the fears and reservations you had at the beginning of the semester.

4. Describe an incident from which you learned an important lesson.

Narrative

5. Write an episode for your favorite television program.

6. Create a new ending for a book or a movie.

7. Relate a conversation you wish you could have with a famous person. Consider someone from either the past or the present.

Process

8. You are working for a large advertising company. Explain the process you would use to introduce a new product.

9. Describe the process you use to prepare a favorite meal or snack.

10. Describe the process you would use to help a new pet become a "member of the family."

Examples

11. Give examples of advertisements that are misleading to the consumer.

12. Give examples of cartoons or other children's TV shows that you feel should be taken off the air.

13. Give examples of some recent fads and explain why they were good or bad.

Comparison/Contrast

14. Compare and contrast two TV programs.

15. Compare and contrast two friends.

16. Compare and contrast the toys you had as a child with the toys you purchase for yourself now.

Persuasive

17. Select any recent controversial subject. Give your opinion and try to persuade the reader to agree with your side on the issue.

18. Should schools be allowed to test students for drugs? Develop a strong case, either for testing or for not testing.

19. Argue for the positive changes you would like to see made in your community, your college, or your local school system.

20. Should college athletes be required to take the same courses as other students to receive a degree or should they be allowed to participate in a program designed especially for the athlete? Write a convincing affirmative answer to one of these questions.

From Sandra K. Hall, Corning Community College, NY

Prewriting

Journal Sheets

- Journal entries, as a prewriting activity, allow a writer to discover ideas. Write freely.

- Grammar and spelling do not count.

- Journal sheets are due at the beginning of the first class of the week.

- Journal entries give writers additional practice with a type of writing.

- Each journal entry should be a page long.

- Journal sheets are worth up to five points each.

- Late journal sheets will receive reduced points.

- You have been given a journal sheet for each week. If you need more room, staple a second sheet on top.

- Return journal sheets that I have seen to your folder—you will need the back of the sheet for a later journal entry.

Sample journal sheets follow.

Name _____

Journal 2

Describe the current state of your desk, your car, your kitchen, or your closet. In the left column, add some sensory details that a person in the class would need to fully picture the scene.

Freewrite:

Comments:

Do you have enough details?

Total earned: _____ /5

Journal 3

Name _____

Describe a person you know very well. Include physical details, behavior, and hints about personality. Your journal sheet will be sealed in a time capsule and read by a relative of this person in the year 2050.

Freewrite:

Comments:

Do you have enough details?

Would this interest the relative?

Total earned: _____ /5

Journal 5

Explain in detail how to do one of these things: eat with chopsticks, iron a shirt, rollerblade, or get to an area landmark from campus.

Name _____

Freewrite:

Comments:

Are the details clear for a beginner?

Have you given enough directions?

Total earned: _____ /5

Journal 7

Write about examples of inexpensive recreation in your area OR movies or songs that contain too much violence OR social problems that concern you. Be sure to be descriptive.

Name _____

Freewrite:

Comments:

Your audience

is: _____

Have you defined inexpensive or

violent?

Do you have enough details?

Total earned: _____ /5

THE WRITING PROCESS:
Moving from Freewriting to Peer Review

Prewriting for Formal Paragraphs and Essays

Early in the assignment period:

- Review the appropriate chapter in the book.

- Do freewriting about a topic, on scrap paper.

- Read over the Planning Sheet for the assignment.

- Complete the Planning Sheet. Do not leave blanks.

- Hand in the Planning Sheet with the final draft.

At the writing stage:

- Write a rough draft from the Planning Sheet. At this point, worry about a topic sentence, organization, details, spelling, sentence structure, grammar, and so forth.

- Only now are you ready for the Peer Review class! (If you do not complete all these steps, and bring a rough draft to class, you are considered UNPREPARED—which equals an ABSENCE!

Planning Sheet for Paragraph #1

Describe an Object

YOUR TOPIC: **YOUR ATTITUDE:**

an unnamed object   It is "useful" or _____.

Brainstorm and freewrite for ten minutes on this topic. Include as many physical characteristics and sensory details as would help identify it. (These include size, dimension, composition, chips in the paint, etc.)

- Now look at the object again, from another angle. Are there any details you have overlooked?

- What seems to be the most important part of the object—the part that you really want to focus on?

- Assume that your AUDIENCE is

  an eleven-year-old who is wired to a Walkman playing heavy metal music, and you have asked him or her to go and get this object.

- Now that you have identified your audience, what does this person need to know about the object?

- What is your PURPOSE in sharing this paragraph with your audience?

  _____ to get that person to find it?

  _____ to get that person to care about that object?

  Other: _____ _____

Moving into the Writing Stage with Paragraph #1

Now, on your *own paper,* write your first draft. Write on one side of the paper and skip lines. **REMEMBER**: A planning sheet is *not a rough draft*!!!!!

CHECKLIST BEFORE PEER REVIEWING

√ Pay close attention to the topic sentence (underline or *highlight* it).

√ Does it immediately grab one's attention? _____

√ Does it introduce a limited topic and attitude toward the topic? _____

√ Do you deliver (in the paragraph) what you promised in the topic sentence? (How will the ten-year-old and the person who peer-reviews the paragraph be able to tell your can opener (e.g.) from the other can openers on the table?) _____

√ Have you arranged these details in a space order that a reader can follow? (See *Evergreen*, pp. 46–50.) When you describe the object, do you jump all around, or move in a logical spatial order? _____

√ Insert transitional words to help this audience follow you—words such as the following. (See *Evergreen*, p. 89)

　　next to, near, close, on top, beneath, left, right center, front, back

√ Does the paragraph have an appropriate closing sentence?

√ Make some beginning revisions as you read it over:

　　Should you add or take out any details or transitional words?
　　Should you change the order of any details?

√ Proofread for errors that you detect.

√ At the top of the rough draft, write a title that *predicts* your topic and attitude.

You are now ready for the Peer Review!

Peer Review—Description: Parag. #1

Writer's name _____ **Reader** _____

Topic: _____ *an object*

Title: _____

---

1. Underline the **topic sentence**. Is it limited enough?

2. Does the opening grab your attention? Why or why not?

---

3. Who is the **audience**?

   _____

   (a general audience or a specific one, such as a family member?)

---

4. What is the central impression being conveyed? (What is the writer trying to communicate?)

---

5. Put a wavy line under any vague words. Discuss with the writer ways to be more *specific*.

Prewriting/Planning: Parag. #3—Process

How to . . .

(See *Evergreen*, pp. 98–107, for help.)

Topic: How to _____

Purpose: To explain a process clearly

Attitude: This process is _____ (easy, important, etc.).

Audience: _____

Criteria: Chronological order; topic sentence must contain a conjunctive adverb; final draft must be done on computer.

BRAINSTORM

Order

✓ Number the steps in chronological order.

✓ Remember your specific audience: have you included all the steps and details he or she needs to follow your explanation?

Rough Draft

On your own paper, write your rough draft. Skip lines.

✓ <u>Underline</u> your topic sentence and make sure it has a **conjunctive adverb**:

Ex. "It is difficult to iron a shirt; **however**, you must follow these steps."

✓ **Proofread** for errors—especially the ones you tend to repeat. (Check your list of strengths/weaknesses.)

✓ Include **transitional words** like *first*, *next*, and *finally* (p. 102).

✓ Make sure you have an encouraging **summary sentence**.

✓ Test your paragraph on a friend: ask the friend to pretend he or she has never eaten spaghetti (e.g.) and to follow your steps in his or her mind. Does the friend get lost or confused at all? *If yes, revise.*

✓ Ask the friend: "Have I made the process clear and interesting? Have I used description to help you follow me? Have I been specific?"

✓ Add a **title** that reveals your topic and purpose.

You are now ready for the Peer Review!

Peer Review: Parag. #3—Process

Writer: _____   *Reader:* _____

Topic: How to _____

Title: _____

     Is it specific? Does it state that the paragraph will explain *how to do something*?

Purpose: To explain a process clearly

Attitude: This process is _____ (easy, important, etc).

Audience: _____

Criteria: Chronological order; topic sentence must contain a conjunctive adverb; final draft must be done on computer.

Topic Sentence

√ Underline the topic sentence.

√ Circle the conjunctive adverb and check for correct punctuation.

     Ex. "It is easy to rollerblade; **however**, you must take certain precautions."

Order

√ Number the steps in chronological order.

√ Has the writer included all the steps and details you need to follow the explanation?

√ Are the instructions **specific** and **detailed**? (Be alert for vague words like *thing* and *thingamajig*.)

√ Has the writer included **transitional expressions** like *first, next,* and *finally*? (102)

√ Has the writer made the process clear and interesting?

Planning Sheet for Parag. #5—Examples

(See *Evergreen*, pp. 86–96)

Final draft must be done on computer and saved!

Topic: To explain, by providing three descriptive examples, the term you defined in Parag. 4.

Topic   _____

Purpose   To explain by examples.

Attitude   These examples are important, to clearly explain:

_____

(Without my examples, some people might confuse stress
with panic, etc.).

Audience   _____

(It helps to imagine your audience as a person in the
Commons who is struggling with this concept to prepare for
a test. How can your examples help?)

Criteria   1. Make sure each example is clear and descriptive.
                 2. Make sure all examples are relevant.
                 3. Arrange them in order from least important to most important.
                 4. Include at least one *complex* sentence. Underline it.

Brainstorm   At least ten minutes on your topic. Generate as many
                 examples as you can—then toss out the weaker ones.

Order

√ Examine the order of your ideas.

√ Remember your specific audience.

√ Have you included all the details and examples your audience needs to follow your explanation?

Moving to the Writing Stage

Rough Draft

On your own paper, write your rough draft. Skip lines.

√ <u>Underline</u> your topic sentence.

√ Proofread for errors—especially the ones you tend to repeat.

√ Make sure you have one **complex sentence**. <u>Underline</u> it.

√ Include **transitions**.

√ Make sure you have a satisfying **concluding sentence**.

√ Test your examples on a friend. Are they clear enough?

√ Ask friend to describe the tone of your paragraph:

_____

(humorous, helpful, serious, sarcastic, sentimental . . .)

√ Add a title that reveals your topic *and* purpose:

    Poor example: A Race Car Fan

    Better example: How to Spot a Racing Car Fanatic

You are now ready for the Peer Review!

Planning Sheet for Essay #1—Comparison or Contrast

(Refer to pages 120–137) for additional help.

Due date for rough draft: Nov. 3

General Topic

Compare or contrast yourself to the way you were five years ago.

Freewrite here about yourself then and now. Include similarities and differences:

Analyze your freewrite.

- Underline points that interest you.
- Can you **categorize** them (for example, changes in appearance, changes in interests)?
- Now decide which you want to focus on: similarities or differences.
- Now, select only the most significant, most interesting similarities or differences and arrange them in two lists:

List A: 5 years ago

List B: Now

Topic

PURPOSE (Am I primarily writing a COMPARISON or a CONTRAST?):

AUDIENCE (Who might read this with interest 25–50 years from now?):

What is the POINT of my comparison or contrast?

Organization

Have I arranged a clear BLOCK pattern of **four** paragraphs?

Have I used clear **transitions**, such as *in contrast, but, however, on the other hand, in addition, similarly*?

Do I set up a clear order within paragraphs 2 and 3 (see p. 257)?

Development

Is each point clear?

        descriptive?

        specific?

Have I selected the *most important* points to compare or contrast?

Are any obvious similarities or differences overlooked?

Outline for Essay #1

Title _____

INTRODUCTION—Parag. 1
THESIS
(Appears at end of ¶ 1)

BODY—Parag. 2	5–7 Sentences Long
TOPIC SENTENCE	

Point 1

Point 2

Point 3

   Are your points in the best order?

BODY—Parag. 3	5–7 Sentences Long
TOPIC SENTENCE	

Point 1

Point 2

Point 3

   Are your points in the best order?
   Do you follow the same order as in parag. 2?

CONCLUSION
What has been the point of your comparison or contrast?

You are now ready for the Peer Review!

Planning Sheet: Persuasion by Cause and Effect

EXIT ESSAY

Rough draft due: **Dec. 13**

Read Ch. 12: pp. 147–161.

SUGGESTED TOPICS:

Because of these reasons (effects), high school sports should be eliminated.

Colleges should require computer literacy courses because of these benefits.

Steuben County's Workfare Program should be ended (or continued) because the program is having these effects:

_____ Your own topic—get it approved by me.

TOPIC Select one of the above, alter it to suit your values, or get another topic approved by me.

_____

Am I arguing for or against? _____

Can *reasonable people* argue the opposite point of view?

Is my topic limited and manageable?

Have I picked a more "middle of the road" position, rather than an extreme one?

AUDIENCE Read pp. 151–152 carefully!

Identify a *specific* audience (such as a person thinking about going to college who does not have any computer skills).

My audience is: _____

This audience also contains 20 people who *strongly disagree* with your position. Describe these people in positive or neutral terms—not negative ones.

(continued on next page)

THE FIVE BASIC METHODS OF PERSUASION pp. 150–151
Use these to support your thesis.

FACTS (What facts can you include? Remember to identify all outside sources!)

1.

2.

3.

Use only *very specific facts*. Do NOT say, "**A lot** of kids are injured every year in team sports, and **many more** lose self-esteem because they weren't picked for the team."

REFERENCE TO AN AUTHORITY

According to _____, _____

EXAMPLES (For instance, how did you feel playing an intense game of basketball, or how did a friend feel starting college without computer skills?)

1.

2.

(Examples, too, need to be **specific and descriptive**).

Do not say, "**Some** of my friends came to college without computer skills and . . ."

Say, "My friend Chris ended up in a freshman English class that required computer skills. She spent 20 hours the first week begging for help in the lab, lost two nights of sleep, and chewed Tums by the handful."

As with *any borrowed information*, *identify sources* that are not from personal experience.

PREDICTING THE CONSEQUENCES (What might happen—positively and negatively—e.g., if sports remain fiercely competitive?)

ANSWER THE OPPOSITION   **CONCESSION**

(Be reasonable here; do not use button pushers like "our kids will grow up to be wimps if we eliminate football.")

Show that you are aware of the opponent's argument, but . . .

(Example: People who are opposed to competitiveness in high school sports are not losers or wimps, but are people seriously concerned about injuries, academics, and good sportsmanship).

(continued)

List their reasons and concerns.

How will you answer their reasonable concerns?

TONE   Your tone must be reasonable.

Avoid name calling and button-pushers.

Avoid extreme positions (such as no sports).

Avoid *you* if at all possible—it puts an audience on the defensive: "If you are in favor of competitive high school sports, you don't care about all the kids injured each year."

THESIS

√ Take a clear position in your thesis. Use *should* if possible.

√ LIST, here and in your thesis, the three *reasons* you have identified as the best ones to support your position.

1.

2.

3.

√ Arrange these reasons in order from **least** to **most important**.

√ Mention them *in your thesis in the same order* in which you plan to cover them in the essay.

Ex. "I agree that safety, academics, and good sportsmanship are important, but there are valid reasons for maintaining a high school sports program."

(continued)

INTRODUCTION

Part I: Lead off with several sentences that introduce your topic.

Part II: State what the opposition believes is important. (Concession)

Part III: Answer the opposition with your thesis:

THESIS _____

_____

Make sure you identify your reasons in your thesis.

PLAN FOR 2nd PARAGRAPH—REASON NUMBER 1

Notes to yourself here. What methods of support can you include?

PLAN FOR 3rd PARAGRAPH—REASON NUMBER 2

What methods of support can you include?

PLAN FOR 4th PARAGRAPH—REASON NUMBER 3

Notes to yourself:

This should be your most important reason.

What methods of support can you include?

What emotional appeals can you fairly include (such as the thrill of victory or pride in doing one's best)?

TRANSITIONS (See p. 150)

CONCLUSION Paragraph 5 (probably)

√ Sum up your reasons.

√ Make a final point.

Do not introduce a new topic such as:

"Teens who are very competitive in school sports go on to be very competitive in life and work."

(If you haven't covered this as a reason, do not throw it in at the end!)

From Sherrie H. Lynch, Andrew College, GA

A Supplemental Exercise for Chapter 1: Writing for Audience

As a supplement to Chapter 1, I add an exercise that students keep in their journals. To reinforce the significance of keeping audience in mind while writing, I ask students to write about events at a recent party, in three separate journal entries: for themselves, for their parents, and for their classmates. Students feel comfortable and are expressive when writing an entry for themselves because I tell them that this entry is "for your eyes only" and that I will not collect it as a part of the journal assignment. After they have written all three entries, I ask volunteers to read the entries for classmates so that they can get immediate feedback from their audience. Finally, we discuss the general differences among the entries, pointing out important concepts such as diction, formality, and appropriateness.

A Supplemental Activity for Chapter 16: A Revising Strategy

After the class reviews Chapter 16 as an introduction to revising, I put the students to work revising their own essays, using the skills highlighted in the chapter. However, I do expand the process somewhat.

First, the students pair off. (They should work with a different partner each time.) Each pair finds a quiet place—an empty classroom, a corner in the hallway, or a bench outside—where each partner will read his or her paper to the other. In doing so, the students can listen for rhythms, determining whether sentences have a variety of structures and lengths. In addition, they can check immediately for surface errors. After an essay is read, the students discuss content concerns: clear thesis, organization, adequate development, unity, and coherence. Following the oral reading and discussion, the partners trade papers and each silently reads the other's paper. Students write in the margins of the essay, pointing out strengths and weaknesses as they see them. Not only are students honing revising skills, they, as readers, are helping the writers focus on the audience's needs and concerns. When students get their papers back with comments and suggestions, they become aware of the back-and-forth work involved in the revising process, and they learn they must decide what revisions they will incorporate in their papers.

From Ann Longknife, College of San Mateo, CA

Writing Process

Students come to us unsure of their ability and often dismayed at finding out how much they do "wrong." In teaching at the developmental level, I have found it extremely important to focus on what they can do and, even more important, to help them see how far they have come. I find the layout of *Evergreen: A Guide to Writing* very helpful.

In the first full class period, I carefully go over Chapter 1, asking questions to make sure the students understand the concepts of subject, audience and purpose. Then I assign a paragraph, using Practice 2, prompt 1. First I ask them to list all the things—both physical and social they have noticed about the college. Then I ask them to write a short essay to fulfill the assignment, first explaining that this is just a practice and not a graded assignment. I also tell them to come and ask me about any spelling or grammar problem. If they know enough to ask, they are already on their way to learning more. I read the essays and make a general comment, pointing out strengths and weaknesses. I also let the students read the essays and then return them to me.

The next classes are spent on a combination of writing and grammar assignments, using the writing chapters in *Evergreen* and parts of the basic grammar section. Students' original essays give me information about where I need to place the greatest grammar emphasis.

A month later I pass out their original essays to let them see what corrections they can make to improve them, and I assign a rewrite. Often my students are amazed at how badly they wrote before and take pride in being able to improve their first efforts so markedly. Again, I am available to answer any questions.

Then, after another month has passed—just before the midterm—I have them do another evaluation and rewrite. This time they discover a lot of things they want to do differently. I grade this effort and it becomes one of the grades for the class. Seldom does anyone get less than a *B*, and that reinforces the message I've tried to make clear—with work and with study, an effort that is not so good can be made much better.

The important outcome of this assignment, made much easier by the way *Evergreen* is set up, is that students discover that they *can* improve their performance and learn *how* they can do it. Then, they know that the decision as to how much time and effort they want to put into their projects is up to them.

From Cliff Gardner, Augusta College, GA

Showing Students How to Revise
to Improve Content Development:

Supplementary Exercise for Chapter 16,
"Putting Your Revision Skills to Work"

Rationale for exercise: Many students find that their writing instructors encourage them to improve the development of their ideas in the body paragraphs of their essays as they revise. This exercise attempts to help students do two things: (1) begin seeing opportunities for elaboration and illustration in paragraphs that have relatively weak development and (2) act on those opportunities by adding specific illustrations and descriptive details to paragraphs.

Writing Sample A

As you read the paragraph below, notice that each of the underlined sentences is a generalization—a sentence that states a point in general terms. There is nothing wrong with the statements made; the problem is that these points may not register in the reader's mind with as much impact as they could with good follow-up examples or descriptive details.

> *My bedroom is my favorite room in my house because it is a place of freedom for me. To some people, having their own bedroom is no big deal. For me, though, it is a privilege because I had to share a room with my older brother for eighteen years. Now that he has moved out, I have a chance to put my own personal mark on the room. While my parents chose to furnish the rest of the house with country decor, I have decided to go with more modern furniture. I've also replaced the pictures on the walls. And now that my brother is gone, I can do whatever I want without being concerned about another person. My bedroom is not just a place where I sleep; it is a place where I make the choices.*

Now read the revised version of the paragraph. Notice the examples and descriptive details added after each underlined sentence to bring each general point to life.

> *My bedroom is my favorite room in my house because it is a place of freedom for me. To some people, having their own bedroom is no big deal. For me, though, it is a privilege because I had to share a room with my older brother for eighteen years. Now that he has moved out, I have a chance to put my own personal mark on the*

(continued)

---

room. *While my parents chose to furnish the rest of the house with country decor, I have decided to go with more modern furniture.* I now have a matte black entertainment center for my stereo, and a formica drawing table instead of my childhood desk. My room is highlighted by matching cylindrical table and floor lamps that have glass discs mounted on top. *I've also replaced the pictures on the walls.* In place of the familiar old landscapes I grew up with, I've hung a wide assortment of framed posters and photographs of people. Now I'm surrounded by a gallery of faces, from the Black Crowes to Courtney Love to a street person from San Francisco. *And with my brother gone, I can do whatever I want without bothering another person.* I sleep when I want, have private telephone conversations anytime I want, and play Nine-Inch Nails with the volume dial set at 8. My bedroom is not just a place where I sleep; it is a place where I make the choices.

Writing Sample B

Step 1: As you read the following paragraph, underline any sentences that you think might be elaborated on in order to add life or emphasis to them. Look for any sentence that makes a point in a general way; imagine how you might bring the statement to life with effective illustration(s) and descriptive details.

    Without a doubt, the waiting room of a doctor's office can be one of the most uncomfortable places in the world. Oh, the seating is not really uncomfortable. However, the chairs are too close together. What makes a waiting room most uncomfortable is being cooped up with strangers who are sick. Also, it's bad enough to run the risk of catching all those different diseases, but when there are badly behaved children sitting across from you, it's hard on the nerves. And the wait seems to go on forever.

Step 2: Now rewrite the paragraph, adding examples and descriptive details after each sentence you underlined above. Remember the purpose of this exercise: **to add life to generalizations in writing by including sharply focused, specific illustrations and descriptions.**

Writing Sample C

In essays, the easiest method of improving content development is to "beef up" the body paragraphs. Read the following essay and follow the same two-step pattern used above: (1) underline in the body paragraphs all the sentences you think might be brought to life with added support; (2) then rewrite the essay, adding sharply focused specific examples and descriptive details after each sentence you underlined.

Make the essay come alive for a reader. With each addition, try to add **impact** and **vividness** to the generalization you are supporting.

Different people have different notions of what constitutes a perfect weekend, of course. As for me, I feel satisfied with my weekends when I've done three important things. Early in the weekend, I like to get the small chores and errands that need to be done out of the way. Another "must" activity for me during any weekend is getting a good physical workout. Most important of all, I need recreation, typically with one or more of my friends.

Before I let myself relax and enter the "fun mode" on Saturday, I always take care of household jobs and run any necessary errands. Every week I have laundry and apartment cleaning to do. Often I listen to music while I clean to make these tasks seem less tedious. I typically go to the grocery store next to get the week's shopping done. Unlike many other people, I enjoy grocery shopping. Sometimes I stop at other stores while I'm out to get more things I need. I try to finish all my chores and errands by mid-afternoon.

After half a day of such duties on Saturday, I want to do something which will get my muscles moving, my heart pumping, and my mind cleared. Exercising fits the bill perfectly. I usually do either of two things: go to the gym or get in a long run. Afterward, I feel a wonderful sense of relaxation.

By Saturday evening, I'm ready for recreation. Often I have a date, but some Saturday nights I go out with a friend or a group of friends. Usually we eat out and catch a movie, although occasionally we spend the evening at one of our apartments. I find that I just don't feel right about a weekend unless I wake up Sunday morning with memories of fun from the night before. On Sunday afternoons, I sometimes like to do some socializing as well.

I use my weekends to get a little work done and to relax. After a good weekend, I feel recharged and ready to meet the world again on Monday morning.

Additional Exercise: Revising One of Your Own Essays

Of course, the focus of the writing course is improving your own writing. When you are writing your own original essays, keep this principle in mind: as you write, look for opportunities to follow up general statements with effective examples and descriptive details. Well-chosen illustrations and details plant ideas more effectively in a reader's mind.

As an exercise, select one of the essays you've already written this term and revise it by

(1) rereading the body paragraphs and underlining any sentences that present ideas in a general fashion only and

(2) rewriting the essay, adding effective examples and descriptive details to enhance your presentation of each idea you underlined.

4

Reviewing Grammar Skills

I have used *Evergreen* longer than any other college text. It provides an excellent balance of instructional material for all areas of emphasis. The layout is very user-friendly for both students and instructors. This is a classic among English composition texts.

Debra O. Callen, Harold Washington College, IL

Evergreen probably has the best treatment of sentence-combining skills available for the beginning writers in English composition courses. *Nobody* doesn't like *Evergreen!*

Michael Douglas, Savanna State College, GA

From Jonathan Dewberry, Interboro Institute, NY

Chapter 29: Prepositions
(Practice Review, pp. 412–413)

The essay concerning Dr. Daniel Hale Williams provides an opportunity to experiment with more than just preposition errors. What I do is take the same essay format and create additional errors, in consistency and parallelism, wordiness, and capitalization. The students have to identify the errors and then rewrite the entire essay. This exercise reinforces accurate proofreading skills as well as grammatical structure and style. My version of the same exercise follows.

GRAMMAR

Directions: Identify the following errors in capitalization, exact language, conciseness, consistency, parallelism, and variety in sentence structure. Rewrite the essay in its corrected version. Proofread carefully for accuracy. (20 pts.)

Dr. Daniel Hale Williams, Pioneer Surgeon

In a lifetime of many successes, dr. Daniel Hale Williams' most greatest achievement was to pioneer open-heart surgery.

young Williams, An african american who grow up in the mid-1800s, knew Poverty. He relied on his wits to get by, becoming, in turn, a shoemaker, then a Musician, and then a barber. At the age of twenty-two, he met Dr. Henry Palmer, who soon see he was capable of becoming a physician. Williams' education, the usual one at the time, in the medical field consisted of a two-year apprenticeship with Dr. Palmer, followed by three years at the Chicago Medical College, where he is specializing in surgery.

It was a good time in medicine science. Surgeons had just started using antiseptics in order to protect and prevent patients against infection. "Dr. Dan," as he was now called, became an experienced expert in the new surgical techniques. "Dr. Dan" became a leader in Chicago's medical and Chicago's African-american communities. In 1891, he succeeds in opening Provident

(continued)

Hospital, the first interracial hospital in the United States for all races. There, African Americans were assured first-rate, top-of-the-line medical care and taken care of. Moreover, black interns and nurses received thorough and complete professional training.

It was to Provident Hospital that frightened friends brought James Cornish on the evening of July 9, 1893. Near death, the young man had received a deep knife gash near his heart during a fight. Dr. Williams decided to operate immediately since he was sensitive to the dangerous situation. According to eyewitnesses, he first made a six-inch incision and removing Cornish's fifth rib. Then, he repaired a torn artery and stitched up the punctured sac surrounding the heart. Fifty-one days later, Cornish left the Hospital, recovered and deeply grateful to Dr. Williams for his life. The age of open-heart surgery had begun.

Much lay ahead for Dr. Williams. He was responsible for reorganizing the Freedmen's hospital at Howard University from 1894 to 1898; in 1913, he accepted an invitation from the american college of surgeons and succeeding in becoming its only African-American charter member. The high point of his life, however, remained that night in 1893.

From June J. McManus, San Antonio College, TX

Correlation with Grammar Computer Lab
on SAC Campus

See the following lab record sheet to observe how I correlated the chapters in *Evergreen* with our grammar program, one designed by a faculty member on our campus.

LAB RECORD

Student Name _____

UNIT IV: Pre-Test (See Post-Test to UNIT IV)		V.1	V.2	V.3	C
Chapter 23, *Evergreen*					
25 1. Sentence Fragment (pp. 338–344)	31				
26 2. Fused (pp. 334–338)	31				
27 3. Comma Splice (pp. 334–338)	31				
28 UNIT IV: Post-Test (pp. 344–345)	31				

UNIT V: Pre-Test (See Post-Test to UNIT V)		V.1	V.2	V.3	C
A. Common Errors: Pre-Test (See Post-Test to UNIT V.A) Chapter 24, *Evergreen*					
29 1. Subj.-Verb Agreement (pp. 346–357)	31				
	51				
30 2. Dangling Modifiers	31				
	51				
31 3. Misplaced Modifiers	31				
	51				
32 4. Faulty Parallelism	31				
	51				
33 5. Confusing Adj. & Adv.	31				
	51				
34 UNIT V.A: Post-Test	31				
	51				

B. Pronoun Errors: Pre-Test (See Post-Test to UNIT V.B)
Chapter 28, *Evergreen*

		V.1	V.2	V.3	C
35	1. Pronoun-Antecedent Agreement: Person, Number (pp. 389–394)	31			
		51			
36	2. Pronoun-Case (usage) (pp. 397–401)	31			
		51			
37	3. Vague Pronoun reference (pp. 394–397)	31			
		51			
38	UNIT V.B Post-Test (pp. 403–404)	31			
		51			

C. Verb Forms: Pre-Test (See Post-Test to UNIT V.C)
Chapters 25, 26, *Evergreen*

		V.1	V.2	V.3	C
39	1. Reg.-Irreg. Principal Parts (pp. 358–362)	31			
		51			
40	2. Active-Passive Voice (pp. 376–378)	31			
		51			
41	3. Tense (pp. 158–163)	31			
		51			
42	4. Errors in 6 Troublesome Verbs (pp. 363–365)	31			
		51			
43	UNIT V.C Post-Test (pp. 356–357)	31			
		51			
44	**D.** Consistency or Unnecessary Shift Problems	31			
		51			
45	UNIT V Post-Test	31			
		51			

Students should complete tests 25–29, 35–43 to finish the lab.

EVERGREEN WITH READINGS

Chapter 23—pp. 334–345
Chapter 24—346–347
Chapters 25, 26—358–378
Chapter 28—389–404

From Patricia Malinowski, Finger Lakes Community College, NY

Grammar Component

For the grammar component, the student could be assigned one or two individual chapters of each unit in *Evergreen* or from a supplemental text such as *Grassroots*. The assignment of these chapters should be based upon the instructor's assessment of the student's weaknesses in writing and grammar. The evaluation of these deficiencies can be continuous during each unit, and the instructor should be ready to supplement weak areas.

The student should be instructed to work through each chapter that has been assigned. Depending on the instructor's preference, the student should self-correct the chapter either section by section or in its entirety. At the conclusion of the chapter, the student should inform the instructor that he or she is ready for a chapter test. Some instructors prefer to confer briefly with the student and check the text responses.

Instructors may wish to specify two chapter-test days per unit and note these on the student calendar. This will enable students to plan and study for these tests and not wait until the last week of a unit to hurriedly complete grammar chapters.

An instructor may decide to handle this grammar component with either whole-class or group/collaborative activities. No matter which strategy is employed, it is important that class and individual study time be used to instruct students in correct grammar usage.

Chapter tests are provided by the publishers of *Evergreen*. These tests are available in the test packet, and there are at least two chapter tests for each grammar chapter.

Instructors should set a specific grade for students to attain for each chapter. A suggested grade for mastery is 80% or better.

From Russ Gaudio, Gateway Community College, CT

What Are My Options?

The options chart (pp. 335–336) illustrating the process of combining sentences in Chapter 22 of *Evergreen: A Guide to Writing,* "Coordination and Subordination," serves as an efficacious teaching tool for instructors of developmental writing and as a visually clear reference guide for basic writing students.

Preparations

After I clearly define and illustrate what a clause is, the difference between one that is independent and one that is dependent, and the role of coordinating and subordinating conjunctions (pp. 324–329). I have students redefine terms, so as to correctly interpret the options chart: the adjectives *coordinate* ("of equal rank or importance") and *subordinate* ("placed in or belonging to a lower order or rank"), and the noun *option* ("the act of making a choice or exercising a preference").

co = equal, with, together

sub = under, beneath (dependent)

ordinate = to put in the same rank or order; to match

options = choices (variety in joining simple sentences and determining relationships between them)

Coordination

Here I engage the class in a Teacher–Question and Class–Answer session on coordination, using the chart (pp. 335–336).

T: What does the box on the left say for Option 1?
C: Independent clause!
T: On the right?
C: Independent clause!
T: If the clause on the left is independent and the clause on the right is independent, what are they?
T/C: Equal and coordinate!
T: What is the process of joining them called?
T/C: Coordination!

We chant the same choral dialogue for Option 2 and Option 3, following the graphic layout that clearly delineates the concepts under study. Since I find that many students (1) place a comma *after* the coordinating conjunction when joining sentences and (2) become generally "baffy" over comma usage in general, I established the "comma so baf-y" rule for Option 1—so that students will remember to place a comma BEFORE *so, b (but),* and *a (and);* and before an *f (for, or, nor)* or *y (yet)* when choosing a coordinating conjunction to establish a relationship between independent clauses.

I help students to easily memorize the first three options by looking at the chart and answering my questions as indicated (it is a given that an independent clause sits on either side of the option).

T: Option 1?
C: Comma so baf-y.
T: Option 2?
C: Semicolon.
T: Option 3?
C: KEEP the semicolon; ADD a conjunctive adverb FOLLOWED by a comma.

Subordination

Now I initiate the next *T*eacher-Question and *C*lass-Answer "vocal," still following our chart (pp. 335–336).

T: What does the box on the left of Option 4 say?
C: Independent clause!
T: What does the box on the right of Option 4 say?
C: Dependent clause!
T: If the clause on the left is independent and the one on the right dependent, what are they?
C: Unequal. One is dependent on the other!
T: What is the process of joining them called?
T/C: Subordination!

We reiterate the same choral rhythms for Option 5 and then begin to review (it is a given here that a subordinating conjunction introduces the dependent clause).

T: Option 4?
C: Independent clause!
T: Followed by?
C: Dependent clause!
T: With?
C: No punctuation!
T: Option 5?
C. Dependent clause!
T: Followed by?
C: Comma!
T: Followed by?
C: Independent clause!

At this point I initiate another question–answer mode for all the options, using fill-in-the-blank types of questions (along with, I confess, Victor Borge punctuation gestures and sounds), saying the answers in unison with the students. It is purposeful pantomime of sights and sounds and gestures.

T: Option 1
C: Comma so baf-y.
T: Option 2
C: Semicolon.
T: Option 3
   Keep the—
C: Semicolon.
   Add a—
C: Conjunctive adverb.
   Followed by a—
C: Comma.

The class enjoys my dog-and-pony show antics but at the same time, learns the options. I then cajole the students to volunteer (almost everyone eventually "wants into" this act) and recite the chart from memory as I roam up and down the aisles asking for options in rapid-fire fashion.

End Results

Finally, students are required to keep a copy of the options chart in a writing folder as an ongoing reference for all remaining writing assignments and class exercises; in this manner, they learn to familiarize themselves with the coordinating and subordinating conjunctions as well as with the conjunctive adverbs. More important, students now have the opportunity to practice, apply, and grasp the serious and powerful mechanisms of coordination and subordination, to add variety to their expression, and to gain a sense of style.

From Ann Longknife, College of San Mateo, CA

How Words Work

One of the techniques I have used is to take the readings—or at least a paragraph or two—and have the students change them—perhaps put everything in past tense, use all past participles, make contractions where none exist. Another technique I have used very successfully, to show how words work and how important changing a word can be, is to have them take a paragraph and find another word for the verb, or adverb, or adjective. They may use a thesaurus, but they still need to be sure the new word does approximately the same thing the old word does.

After they have changed the words, I have them put a couple of sentences on the board and we discuss which choice was best and why. This gives them the exercise of finding the new word, seeing what new words others have chosen, and how each of these word changes has altered what is being said. They really begin to see what a difference even a subtle change or a slightly different word can make.

From Ann L. Lathrop, Lehman College, NY

Grammar and Mechanics

In the first two weeks at the beginning of the semester, before a more detailed review, I give an overview of the parts of speech and sentence functions (subject, object, subject complement, verb or predicate, etc.) so that the students and I have a common metalanguage with which to discuss their writing and the explicit grammar lessons that will follow. I then use the chapters on grammatical structures and mechanics (21–33) as a general review for the class and on an as-needed basis for students experiencing difficulty with specific structures. ESL students also need supplementary work concerning articles, modals, gerunds, infinitives, and prepositions.

5

Writing
Paragraphs
and Essays

The balance between paragraph development and composing short essays in *Evergreen* allows instructors to tailor this text to their individual methods of teaching composition. I emphasize entire essays. Other instructors place more emphasis on practice with individual paragraph construction. Instructors who design composition courses with widely divergent emphases find the text eminently satisfying.

John Thornburg, San Jacinto College, TX

I think the balance of paragraph/short essay writing is well designed. Since the authors provide lists of possible topics for writing in each strategy, the instructor can easily decide on the number of assignments appropriate to the capability of any particular class: sometimes emphasizing paragraphs, at other times spending more time on essays.

Muriel M. Brennan, College of San Mateo, CA

From June J. McManus, San Antonio College, TX

Writing Assignment: Paragraph

Because the print in *Evergreen* is not in color, I introduce the writing project by bringing in a similar Frida Kahlo painting borrowed from a friend to give the students an idea of Kahlo's color tones. On that day, as a class activity, students volunteer several dominant impressions (nature, friendship, exotic, wild, tropical, for example) of the painting in *Evergreen*, and the class chooses one impression to brainstorm and cluster as a class project (I do not offer suggestions). When they write their papers, they may select the impression we worked on in class, or they may choose different impressions.

This has been an excellent technique for teaching analytical thinking and organizational skills.

Writing Assignment: Paragraph

Topic: Frida Kahlo's self-portrait, p. 40 in *Evergreen*. You should use your book and the notes I gave you on the clustering technique.

Instructions:

1. Select one word for the dominant impression the painting makes on you. Make that word your title.

2. Write a topic sentence focusing on your dominant impression and begin your paragraph with that sentence.

3. Continue your paragraph, developing a description of the painting in an organized way to provide the dominant impression.

4. Revise your paragraph, edit it for errors, and recopy it neatly.

5. Turn in all drafts at our next class meeting, with final draft on top. Endorse your paper as instructed.

From Robert Mann, Urban Campus, Des Moines Area Community, IA

The Party: A Variety of Exercises

Here is one exercise I have invented that works in a number of ways. This exercise may be applied to the following *Evergreen* chapters.

Chapter 1, "Exploring the Writing Process" (Subject, Audience, and Purpose, especially)
Chapter 5, "Illustration"
Chapter 6, "Narration"
Chapter 7, "Description"
Chapter 8, "Process"

Background for the students:

"Imagine there has been a big party on your block. There are cars parked everywhere. The music is really loud. There are people wandering over lawns neighboring the party house. The police are called by one of the neighbors. The police arrive. Arguments pop up. Some people are arrested."

Assignment: For Chapter 1, instructor to students:

"I am going to divide you into groups. You are to pretend you are one of the people at the scene of this party. Group A will be partygoers. Group B will be neighbors. Group C will be police. Now the police arrive. Let's start this scene. What would you most likely be saying, neighbors?"

After the role-playing, lead a discussion of differences in viewpoints and presentations of the scene—in all possible varieties: vocabulary, selection of detail, order of presentation of support, and so on that are logically possible. What differences in purpose would the groups at this scene have and how would they be likely to demonstrate them? What are the differences in audience these groups would interpret and, again, how would these differences be shown? List these differences in some fashion on the chalkboard, as an example, so that students get an idea of interrelatedness, of language, and organization.

Assignment: For Chapters 5 through 8, instructor to student, *re* this same scenario:

"Write a _____ (narrative, process, and so on) paragraph of the scene, pretending you are a police officer or a neighbor or a partygoer. Write to _____ (mother, friend, fulfill requirements of reporting). How does your choice of _____ (formality/informality, word choice, etc.) vary?"

From Ann L. Lathrop, Lehman College, NY

A Follow-Up Lesson:
Chapter 3, Parts D, E, and F

To prepare students for expanding their writing from paragraphs into essays, I often use the song "Trash" recorded by The Bobs as a follow-up lesson to Chapter 3, Parts D, E, and F (pp. 31–38). Students enjoy the change of pace and medium, and ESL students especially appreciate having a script of the lyrics to refer to after they have tried to catch the main idea and the meaning after the first playing. The topic, messiness, is humorously appealing and easily recalls the earlier lesson involving the evidence of Pete's sloppiness.

The stanza form illustrates paragraphing and linkage to a basic theme or main idea. Each stanza begins with a reference to an adage (the topic sentence), develops that theme using lexical collocations (castle—royalty, queen, heart—cardiac arrest, care; godliness—heathen, heretic, altar, collection plate), and has a conclusion. The overall conclusion presents an extreme solution to the problem, but one that the listener has been prepared for. The lack of an introduction is a good point for discussion, and students working in small groups can try to write an appropriate opening. The instructor can also point out dialect (the use of the double negative: "I can't get no rest") and orthographic ("gonna") register differences if the students do not question their use.

Students talk with great animation about the irksome habits of roommates or spouses, and these discussions provide the basis for especially lively essays. Other related successful writing assignments involve strategies for getting rid of an unwanted roommate, the proper behavior for keeping peace with one's roommate, or proverbs from students' home cultures that students can apply to a central theme and fully develop with translations and explanations of the context in which they are uttered, their purposes, and their effects—all of which build on the model of the original paragraph from the textbook or the lyrics of the song and lead students easily toward full-length and well-formed essays.

From Sandra K. Hall, Corning Community College, NY

Moving from a Paragraph to an Essay:
Evergreen, pp. 242–245

To understand the difference between the paragraph and essay, I augment pp. 269–70 of *Evergreen* with this material.

Acting to Save Mother Earth

Every day we hear more bad news about our planet. What can we do in the face of such widespread gloom? **We can each learn practical ways to better our environment.** For example, saving and recycling newspapers has a number of positive results. Another Earth-saving habit is "precycling" waste. Wise management of hazardous household waste is yet another way of taking action for the planet. These personal actions may not seem important, but if carried out on a larger scale, they could greatly improve our environment and our lives.

The above paragraph contains three examples (circled) and uses transitions. Nevertheless, what problems do you see with trying to cover the topic in one paragraph?

From Ann Richey, Interboro Institute, NY

Writing Exercises: Transitions

To help students understand the role of transitions in writing, I sometimes take an editorial from the *New York Times,* photocopy it, and cut it into paragraphs (and, where instructive, smaller meaningful units). I give each student an envelope with the "puzzle pieces" and require that the article be reassembled. In addition to demonstrating the importance of transitions in logical coherence, this project also enhances the students' sense of essay organization by forcing them to distinguish the likely opening paragraph(s), thesis statement, development, and conclusion. This exercise can be made increasingly challenging over the semester by, for example, picking an editorial with its thesis stated at the end, or an editorial where the thesis must be inferred.

From Susan VanSchuyver, Oklahoma City Comunity College, OK

Descriptive Writing

Resources

Chapter 7, "Description"
Chapter 15, "Revising for Language Awareness"

Type of Activity

Introductory Group Activity

Objectives

To introduce word choice, audience, and descriptive language
To promote creativity in the use of language

Directions

1. Decide how many small groups you will need to divide the class into groups of three to four students. Assemble at least five different colors of lipstick, markers, or crayons, and white paper. Draw a thick slash of each color on each sheet of paper and number each slash. Make enough pages that each small group has a page with five numbered slashes of color.

2. As a total group, well-known and overused discuss descriptive phrases used for colors: fire-engine red, lemon yellow, sky blue. Discuss the need to appeal to the senses and to interest the audience.

3. Give each group one of the sheets of paper with the five slashes of color. Tell the students that they must create a name for each color with a word or phrase that would make a customer want to purchase that lipstick or marker or crayon. Introduce the idea of appealing to the specific audience (customer).

4. After the groups have had time to name their colors (10–15 minutes), write the names on the marker board or use an overhead projector. First write down the names of the number one color from each group. Compare and discuss. Point out truly creative word choices. Continue for color two and so on.

Outcomes

Students will have a better understanding of audience; they will have a foundation for beginning to write descriptive sentences (Chapter 18) and paragraphs (Chapter 7).

From Keysha Ingram-Gamor, Montgomery College, MD

Description, Comparison, and Process Assignments

Description

I try to encourage the use of all senses in this unit. To achieve that, I usually conduct an activity that I call "Sense Stations: Painting Pictures with Words."

Before setting up the sense stations, I give a talk about the importance of description in any writing for any purpose. We discuss two ways of describing, objectively and subjectively. I have been surprised by how well the students understand how to distinguish between the objective description and the subjective description. Students generally do a fantastic job of deciding when and why each approach is appropriate. After analyzing the effects of figurative language in our readings and class activities, students are excited about painting their own pictures with words. I have found, too, that students love to explore their use of figurative language during this project. They are usually eager to share their stories. In my experience, this activity has proven to be one that students enjoy and remember.

I set up in the classroom stations or sections wherein the use of one sense is dominant. A station for each of the five senses is crucial, and I leave instructions at each station so that students will know what is expected. I encourage (require) each student to take notes as the observation is occurring, for these details will suffice as information gathering. When the student's two-minute visit is up, he or she will write a brief paragraph describing the experience. In the end, the students will write a story using all the details they experienced while visiting each station. Having students who are unable to experience a particular station—the auditory station, for example—proves to be a valuable lesson for the entire class regarding the importance of a variety of approaches or appeals. Some station suggestions:

Try to help students have a variety of stories they could create. Students need only to complete the paragraphs of the stations they plan to use in their stories, but it's crucial that they gather information at all stations.

Many times students are unfamiliar with the station names. Teachers are presented with an opportunity to work in some key root words.

I. Ocular
  A. Collage—allows personal experience to dictate what the student sees
  B. Picture—of an object, a historical figure, a place, or whatever you like
  C. Object

II. Auditory
  A. Sounds one hears at night in the country or city
  B. Different types of music
  C. Sounds heard during different weather situations

   III. Olfactory
         A. Sweet—perfume or flowers
         B. Foul—chemical, animal, or other
         C. Nature—seasonal associations; i.e., evergreens evoking thoughts of
             winter

   IV. Tactile
         A. Sand or sandpaper
         B. Wet (something wet or something cold or warm)
         C. Brittle—dry leaves
         D. Squishy—dough or cooked noodles

    V. Palatal
         A. Salty
         B. Sweet
         C. Bitter
         D. Spicy (whatever you choose—try to target every part of the tongue)

Comparison and Contrast

   I. *Let's Make a Deal!*
       I have students compare their two textbooks for class. Their goal is to
       convince me to discontinue assigning material from one of the texts. If they
       are successful at writing thoughtful statements indicating pros and cons
       of each text, in the end—supporting their choice—I will give them a break
       from homework taken from that textbook, for some predetermined period.

  II. I assign students to write a paper explaining why this paper is going to be
       better (not repeating the same errors) than the last one.

Process

   I. I have students analyze three articles on the same subject, in an effort to
       study fact and opinion, then write a paper about how they approached this
       analysis.

  II. I write different locations, all on campus, on a piece of paper and tear the
       paper into pieces so that one location is on each sliver. Students select a
       piece out of a bowl. Their task is to give someone directions from the desig-
       nated point on campus to their classroom. They cannot forego context—
       explaining the purpose, indicating an audience, and so on. Students really
       enjoy this one. They should be encouraged to go out and walk through the
       process, taking notes along the way. This assignment can be completed as
       an in-class writing assignment.

From Angela L. Chilton, Tarrant County Junior College, Northwest Campus, TX

Developing Persuasive Essays

One of the biggest writing problems our remedial students face is development—this refers not to methods of using the facts in their knowledge base, but to their having a very limited knowledge base concerning local, state, national, and world issues.

To remedy this shortcoming, I requested from our Houghton Mifflin representative videotapes usually reserved for history, government, psychology, and sociology. In class, our writing students receive a persuasive writing prompt and we collaboratively brainstorm for examples. This session usually results in students' being able to state their opinions but unable to support them, due to lack of examples and specifics. Responding to this need immediately, we watch a video on a related topic and take notes. When we finish the videotape, we again collaboratively list examples, augmenting our previous list with real and specific details. The students then have much more information and a greater opportunity to write a passing essay. At the next class meeting, the students write an in-class essay using that information; they do not use their notes (since the TASP test, for which they are preparing, allows no such reference materials). With this plan, they incorporate the information into their knowledge base and exercise their memory faculties.

With this method, our students overcome knowledge deficits, one topic at a time. They also comment that writing is much easier when they know what to say. This encourages them to become more aware by watching or listening to news programs and reading more newspapers and news magazines. Students become more alert to issues and often see opportunities to become involved in the issues we cover in class. They also develop a respect for the need and benefit of research as a part of the writing process. Here are some sample video programs and writing prompts.

Prompt:

Should the federal government regulate the environmental impact of businesses? Proponents believe that businesses will damage the environment with toxic waste unless the government imposes and enforces safe standards. Opponents believe that businesses should regulate themselves without further federal interference.

Your assignment is to write an essay, 300–600 words, to be read by a classroom instructor, in which you support one side of this argument. Be sure to use appropriate reasons and examples to defend your stance.

Related Video:

The Environmental Protection Agency. Illustrates the various forms of pollution, their causes, and the creation of the Environmental Protection Agency.

Prompt:

Who should be the ultimate authority for interpreting the U.S. Constitution: the Supreme Court or a majority vote of U.S. citizens? Some believe that Supreme Court justices are more knowledgeable and experienced in matters of constitutional rights. Others believe that the Supreme Court is too political, basing decisions primarily on Republican and Democratic platforms.

Your assignment is to write an essay, 300–600 words, to be read by a classroom instructor, in which you support one side of this argument. Be sure to use appropriate reasons and examples to defend your stance.

Related Video:

The Supreme Court. Details the Webster Case, illustrating the division on the abortion issue between Supreme Court decisions and state regulations.

From Jonathan Dewberry, Interboro Institute, NY

Chapter 17
"The Process of Writing an Essay"

Based it on the essay composition section, I provide an *outline* for the students to follow with all of their essays. This assists them in organizing their ideas better, understanding connections between ideas, and condensing information into a main idea/subpoint format. Indeed, this outline parallels the structure of all the essays in Chapter 18, "Types of Essays." It further illustrates how essays, despite diversity in type, (narrative, descriptive, classification, comparison-contrast), still adhere to the same structural foundation in composition.

TITLE

Thesis Statement: (Central idea in *one* sentence only)

I. Introduction
   A. Attention-getter
   B. Thesis statement introduced

II. Body
   A. Main idea (topic sentence)
      1. Subpoint
         a.
         b.
      2. Subpoint
         a.
         b.
   B. Main idea (topic sentence)
      1. Subpoint
         a.
         b.
      2. Subpoint
         a.
         b.
   C. Main idea (topic sentence)
      1. Subpoint
         a.
         b.
      2. Subpoint
         a.
         b.

III. Conclusion
   A. Summary
   B. Concluding statement

From Anne Richey, Interboro Institute, NY

LESSON PLAN
Evergreen, Chapter 12
"Persuasion"

Introducing Persuasion

To introduce persuasion and to make argumentative writing seem less daunting to my students, I often begin with a hypothetical case or situation that requires the students to provide solid evidence which could be used to support our chosen position. This discussion *precedes* our examination of Chapter 12. I keep the issue noncontroversial so that our deliberations stay on track—we are marshaling evidence, not debating the issue. I write my students' suggestions on the board. Usually they come up with facts, examples, predictions, authorities, and sometimes answers to the opposition. With the occasional less imaginative class, I prompt them. Once we have 10–12 very specific points on the board, I note the types of evidence discussed on pp. 148–149 in Chapter 12, write them on the board, and then ask the students to classify their ideas according to those types. They are always pleasantly surprised to see they're already adept at using argumentative evidence. "This, I say, is not something I have to teach you, for you do it in your daily lives every time you have an argument or discuss an important issue. My job," I continue, "is to help you be more aware of the methods of support you use and to point out their strengths and pitfalls." From there we get into detailed discussion of argumentation. When I assign their essays, I require students to use at least three types of evidence and to label them in the margin.

Chapter 12, "Persuasion," as a Basis for the Research Paper

This semester, I am trying a new approach to term paper writing. I am requiring that my EN 101 students base their research papers on an argumentative essay. This approach, I hope, will enable students to see that research has a practical application and that it can not only buttress a presentation but also enlarge it. My plan is to have them write their required persuasive essay, choosing from a list of fifteen topics that I know inspire strong opinions and whose treatment does not require much more than common sense and experience—at least in this first stage. Once the essays are graded, I will require that the students use them as the foundation of their research papers. At this point, they will be expected to begin their research, looking for facts, examples, predictions, authorities, and statistics that they can integrate into their essays to make them more convincing. Along the way, I will guide them on the use of bibliography cards, note-taking, library use, documentation, and so forth. When I collect the papers, I will keep my fingers crossed that this time I'll be reading work that reflects conviction, some real footwork, and the students' voices.

6
Suggested Writing Topics

The discussion and writing questions following each reading are exceptionally well done. They impressed me as thoughtful and engaging. They do an exceptionally good job of separating the questions into "levels," with the questions for discussion involving recall and moving to some analysis, and the writing assignments inviting students to synthesize and be creative.

Linda Whisnant, Guilford Community Technical College, NC

Evergreen's strongest plus for me has been the writing assignments based on photographs, and those at the end of each reading. They inspire creativity and evoke students' interest in one another's responses; class members become willing, even eager, to read their papers aloud. Lively discussions ensue.

Margaret Koenig, Monterey Peninsula College, CA

From Sherrie H. Lynch, Andrew College, GA

Specific Writing Assignments
from *Evergreen*

1. Describe a room in your home. Describe one that is special to you—the bedroom, the kitchen, or the den. Choose details that capture that special feeling of the room. Be sure to organize the details in space order before you begin to write the rough draft.

2. Describe a photograph. Describe the one I have provided you, as clearly as you can. First, jot down several important details in the scene. Then arrange these details in some sort of space order. Do this prewriting before you begin your rough draft.

3. Study the photographs that I gave you of the two couples. Look carefully at their facial features and expressions, at their body language, at their clothing, and at their surroundings. Compare and contrast the two couples. First, jot down the similarities and differences you see. Ask yourself a few questions: What is my general impression of each pair? How do they seem to be getting along? How are the couples alike and how are they different? Do your prewriting before you begin your rough draft.

Evaluation Assignments

Unit I — Evaluation

Write a clear and well-developed paragraph on one of the following topics. Remember to narrow the topic, write the topic sentence, brainstorm, and select and arrange your ideas before you write your rough draft and your final draft. HAND IN ALL WORK.

1. At some time, we have all accomplished something either at work or at school that we are proud of. Describe an accomplishment you are proud to have achieved.

2. We often find ourselves being in the wrong place at the wrong time, or saying the wrong thing. This leads to embarrassing situations. Describe an embarrassing incident in your life.

3. People are an important influence in our lives. Describe several ways in which someone has influenced your life. Remember that influences can be positive or negative.

Unit II — Evaluation

Select ONE of the following topics and develop it into a mini-essay. Make sure you have an introduction, a middle paragraph (or paragraphs), and a conclusion. You should hand in all your work: brainstorming, organization, rough draft, and final draft.

Topics:

1. Illustration (examples)—People who have overcome handicaps, poverty, prejudice, and so on

2. Descriptive—The effects of a rainstorm or snowstorm

3. Narrative—An experience in which you were embarrassed or disappointed

4. Cause and effect—Why so many young students are afraid of school

Unit III — Evaluation Essay

Write an essay of four or more paragraphs on one of the following topics. Include an outline, first draft, and final draft.

1. Describe the things that you would change in your community and why.

2. You are one of the last people of your generation on earth. Select three items that you would leave for future generations. Defend your choices.

3. The law has made the use of seat belts mandatory in the state of New York. Do you agree, or disagree, with the law?

4. Does television serve a purpose or is it just the "boob tube"? Explain your opinion.

Unit III — Alternate Evaluation Essay

Select one of the following topics. Write an essay in which you give an affirmative or a negative response to the question. Your essay should consist of an introduction in which you have a clear thesis statement, at least three paragraphs that support your thesis, and a conclusion.

1. Should there be mandatory testing for AIDS?

2. Should people with AIDS be allowed in the workplace? to attend school?

3. Should people who knowingly transmit AIDS be liable to criminal prosecution?

4. Should health care professionals (doctors, nurses, lab technicians) have the right to refuse to work with AIDS patients?

5. Should the government (local, state, or federal) sponsor programs in which clean needles are given to drug addicts in exchange for old needles?

6. Should a hospital be held liable if a patient contracts AIDS during a hospital stay or from a blood transfusion?

From Jane Wilson, Ivy Tech State College, IN

Paragraph Writing Assignments

Chapters 5–12 on paragraph styles provide rich opportunities for in-class writing assignments. These writing assignments change from semester to semester; the listing below is only a sample of topics used.

1. **Illustration**

   What is your favorite TV show, and why? Use examples.

   How do you successfully study for a test? Use examples.

2. **Narration**

   (Please see my original submission.)

3. **Description**

   You have just heard Thoreau's description of Walden Pond. Describe the area for me in your own words.

   Describe the car of the future, as you see it.

   Describe your favorite place. Invoke all the sensory images that apply.

   Describe a specific table in the classroom in such detail that I will be able to find it among all the others.

4. **Process**

   Tell me how to accomplish a task you know well; pay particular attention to including all necessary details and steps.

5. **Comparison/Contrast**

   Read these short biographical sketches of two individuals and compare and/or contrast them.

For the comparison/contrast writing assignments, I provide the biographical sketches, in my own words, and we discuss possible criteria for evaluation. I also bring in samples of my own or student writing on various topics and ask the students to analyze them.

From Anne Richey, Interboro Institute, NY

Argumentative Essay/Research Paper Topics

1. Day care—effects on children
2. Television violence—effects on children/viewers in general
3. Exercise—its importance for mental and physical health
4. Abortion—parental permission for teens
5. Gangsta rap—images of women reflected in it
6. Teenage suicide—causes
7. Organ transplants—who gets them and when
8. Crash helmets for motorcyclists—mandatory or not?
9. Doctor-assisted suicide—legal or not?
10. College athletes—exploited by their schools?
11. Automation—should there be limits when jobs are at stake?
12. Animals—do they have feelings?
13. Ultrathin models—effects on young girls' self-images
14. Juvenile delinquency—Should parents be the ones who are punished?
15. Athletes—steroid use

From Susan McKnight, Tarrant County Junior College, TX

Sample TASP Writing Assignments

Assignment 2(a)

Are professional athletes paid too much? Some people feel that athletes are paid too much, receiving multimillion dollar contracts just for playing a game. Others feel that the huge salaries players receive are only their fair share of the billions of dollars the owners receive from concessions and television rights.

Your purpose is to write a multiple-paragraph essay, between 300 and 600 words, to be read by a group of National Football League owners. You take a position on whether or not professional athletes are overpaid. Be sure to defend your position with logical arguments and appropriate examples.

Assignment 2(b)

Should the United States prison system abolish parole? Proponents of this idea believe that abolishing parole would reduce the crime rate. Opponents think that parole works; inmates work harder at reform and good behavior if they know they will be rewarded with parole.

Your purpose is to write a multiple-paragraph essay, between 300 and 600 words, to be read by the National Board for Prison Reform. You take a position on whether or not the prison system should do away with parole. Be sure to defend your position with logical arguments and appropriate examples.

From Jane Wilson, Ivy Tech State College, IN

BSA 025
Intro to College Writing II

Persuasive Essay Topics

Choose one of the following as the topic for your persuasive essay.

1. Argue for or against giving your all to "getting ahead." Do the benefits of hard work (money, security, status, and so on) outweigh the disadvantages (pressure, loneliness, lack of free time, and so on)? Is "getting ahead" worth the time and effort it takes?

2. In today's world, many wives in two-parent families must work outside the home in order for the family to "make ends meet." Should husbands of wives who work outside the home help with the housework and child care?

3. It is a fact of life that drug addiction exists in our society. While the ultimate goal would be to wipe out such addiction, that will take time. In the meantime, many addicts share needles used to inject the drugs. This sharing of needles is one of the identifiable causes of the spread of AIDS. Should sterile needles be provided to addicts (at taxpayers' expense) to help halt the spread of AIDS?

4. Ivy Tech's mission is to give students specific skills that will enable them to compete successfully in today's job market. However, one of the skills required for being successful in most jobs is the ability to deal with people, whether coworkers or clients. Sociology is the study of how people interact. Should sociology be a required course at Ivy Tech?

5. Music changes from one generation to the next. My parents didn't enjoy the music I did when I was growing up. I don't enjoy all of the music my children listen to. Is popular music today more or less exciting than the music of ten (or twenty) years ago?

6. For many years, the legal system has based decisions on adoption rights on the assumption that only two-parent families are equipped to deal with the pressures of raising children. Today, many individuals are challenging that assumption. Should single people be allowed to adopt children?

7. There is a great deal of controversy today about proper penalties for those convicted of driving while intoxicated. What do you feel the punishment should be for those convicted of drunk driving?

7

Writing Research Papers

A mini research paper if a scholarly activity which involves all the processes of preparing a research study: topic identification, investigating source material, preparing research cards, developing a bibliography. . . . It is the first step of scholarship.

William G. Thomas, Los Angeles Trade Technical College, CA

From Sandra K. Hall, Corning Community College, NY

Research 11:
Information Superhighway

Name _____   Grade _____

Due ___*Nov. 13*_____

Planning a Research Essay (Essay 2)

STEP 1: Review your note cards and the highlights on articles.

What interests you? _____

What do you have enough information on that would develop into a good paper?
(Examples of? Causes of? etc.)

_____

So, my <u>narrowed</u> FOCUS is: _____

_____

My PURPOSE is: _____

STEP TWO: Determine a specific audience: _____

STEP THREE: Go back to your notes and select the cards that have useful information.
Arrange the cards in a logical order.
Are you missing any important information? (If so, go find it!!)

STEP FOUR: Jot down some notes here that you want to remember for your conclusion.

_____

_____

_____

OUTLINE Also on disk (Res. 9)

This is just a model. You will need to change this outline to fit the purposes you identified on previous page.

Title: _____

PARAGRAPH 1:   Intro

- Make several statements that introduce us to the topic and get our attention.
- State your *thesis* as the last sentence.

PARAGRAPH 2:   Body Paragraph — your evidence

- Supporting detail #1
- Supporting detail #2
- Supporting detail #3

PARAGRAPH 3:   Additional Body Paragraphs — as needed

- Supporting detail #1
- Supporting detail #2
- Supporting detail #3

CONCLUSION:

- What do we do with the information we have just read?
- Why is it important? (Etc.)

You are now ready to get Res. 11 approved and start writing your rough draft.

Remember that the rough and the final drafts will need a Works Cited page, to be complete (this is Res. 7).

FROM IDEA
to
LIBRARY SEARCH
to
ARTICLES on topic
to
NOTES
to a
RESEARCH PAPER

 Information Superhighway

LIBRARY PRINTOUT:

Access No.   02295365
Title: A new divide between haves and have-nots?
Journal: Time (GTIM)
              Vol. 145 Iss. 12 Date: Spring 1995 p. 25–6
Subjects: Information Superhighway; Computers;
              Social Classes

NOTECARD:

Author: *Ratan*

page: *25*

_____ Quote   _✓_ Paraphrase   _____ Own idea

Americans are spending almost as much on computer purchases as they are on televisions.

ARTICLE:

[TEXT]

PAPER:

Most American families own television sets, but, what is surprising is the growing number of families who are buying computers. In fact, they are purchasing nearly an equal number of computers (Ratan 25). About 8 billion computers were sold in 1994. . . .

WORK CITED:

Ratan, Suneel. "A New Divide Between Haves and Have-nots?" *Time* Spring, 1995. 25–26.

MAKING SENSE OF LIBRARY PRINTOUTS:
How to Create a Works Cited List
in MLA Style

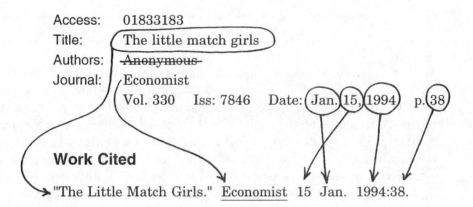

Access: 01833183
Title: The little match girls
Authors: Anonymous
Journal: Economist
            Vol. 330   Iss: 7846   Date: Jan. 15, 1994   p. 38

Work Cited

"The Little Match Girls." Economist 15 Jan. 1994:38.

Remember: If there is no author, start with the title.
                Use " ".
                Capitalize significant words.

                Use (F8) to underline titles of magazines and books.
                Indent second and third lines if any part of the information
                  extends beyond one line. (Use TAB)

                If the magazine or paper is published weekly or daily, don't
                forget to put date before the month.

From Jane Wilson, Ivy Tech State College, IN

BSA 025
Research Paper

Selecting a Topic

The first step in writing a research paper is selecting a topic. The topic should be one that interests you, one that you wish to learn about. Most topics initially considered are too broad to fit the requirements of the paper and must be narrowed in scope. For example, the topic of "Sports" would be too general. You would need to narrow your subject to deal with a specific sport or with a specific happening in the world of sports. Once the topic is narrowed, ideas must be generated and organized. You might wish to refer to Chapters 2 and 3 in *Evergreen* for a review of how to generate and group ideas. The final step in this planning is the creation of a focused, directed thesis statement, and this must, of course, be a grammatically correct and clear sentence or group of sentences.

Topic (general) _____

Narrowed Topic _____

Idea Generating and Organizing Show this work on a separate, attached sheet.

Thesis Statement _____

Research Paper
BSA 025
Intro to College Writing II
Summer, 1995

1. The research paper will be 5–6 pages long (this includes the text of the paper but does *not* include the Works Cited page).

2. The paper must be double-spaced.

3. The paper must have margins of approximately one (1) inch on all sides.

4. There will be no cover page, only an appropriate heading on the first page of the paper.

5. The material presented in the paper should be gathered from at least 5 sources.

    a. Only 1 encyclopedia may be used.

    b. Use recent material, when possible.

    c. Materials may include books, magazines, reference books, pamphlets, videos, audiocassettes, interviews, newspapers, and so forth.

6. The Works Cited page and parenthetical reference should be according to the MLA format of documentation.

7. The paper will require the creation and submission of fifty (50) notecards.

8. The final draft of the research paper must strive for accuracy of information, documentation, presentation, and grammar.

From William Thomas, Los Angeles Trade Technical College, CA

An Initiation into Research in English

DESCRIPTION: Re-search means to look again at a problem, topic, or subject of interest with new eyes, with a new mind putting information together. It requires that references be utilized and cited, or given credit as sources. It is the first step of scholarship—to seek truth or confirmation of hypotheses or facts to support a premise. It is not copying information indiscriminately and pretending the words are yours (this is a no-no . . .).

A mini research paper is a scholarly activity that involves all the processes of preparing a research study: topic identification, investigating source material, preparing research cards, developing a bibliography, identifying appendices, and utilizing the Modern Language Association guidelines in organizing your study. All of the essential elements of a research study are present, except that instead of preparing 60 to 100 pages of research information, you need only prepare sample pages with examples of footnoting and citations on a footnote reference.

TOPICS: Topics may be of your own choosing. Suggested ideas include:

- An aspect or characteristic of a culture other than your own, represented by another student; religion, food, favorite sports, educational system, major products, and so forth.

- A current event such as, for instance, the abortion issue, the presidential campaign, racism in television, the war on drugs, or equal educational opportunity.

- A new invention or product for which you may want to predict a future—such as something relating to television, mini-helicopters, wristwatch radios, lasers, sonar, pacemakers, or an item of your choice.

LENGTH: Mini research papers should be five to eight pages, double-spaced, typewritten, or word-processed.

FOOTNOTES: When you quote a source such as a book, magazine article, or interview, you should indicate that with a number beginning with "1" at the point of citation in your narration. In the appendices of your research paper, you should present the citation following the appropriate number on one or more pages titled "Footnotes." Listing such footnotes indicates that yours is a research paper, because you have sought out other materials relating to your topic of study.

BOOK, ARTICLE, OR INTERVIEW SOURCE FORMAT:

Book

Brown, Sam (Author), <u>Rio Bravo: The Great River</u> (Book), Bantam Books (Publisher), 1995 (Date), p. 123 (Specific source page).

Article in Book

Johnson, George (Author), "The Rolly Polly," (Article), <u>Being Plump</u> (Book in which article appears), Frankenstein & Sons (Publisher), 1823 (Date), p. 23 (Specific source page).

Article in Magazine or Newspaper

Albert, Frankie (Author), "Breaking the Fast Break" (Article), Sportsnotes (Magazine), July 7, 1989 (Date), Volume I, Number 7 (Specific publication), p. 87 (Specific source page).

Interviewee

Ho, Ron (Interviewee), Los Angeles Trade Technical College Student from Korea (Validation as expert on subject), February 4, 1991 (Date of interview).

or

Watkins, Johnathon, M.D. (Interviewee), Director of Abortion Clinic, USC Medical Center (Validation as expert on subject), January 23, 1990 (Date of interview).

BIBLIOGRAPHY: The bibliography includes all sources investigated, whether or not quotes or footnotes are used. Even if you just thumbed through a book to see if it would be helpful, list it.

Organization of Paper

Title Page: Format

Title of Paper
Your Name
Date
Class

"In partial fulfillment of the requirements of the class of English 101, Dr. Wm. G. Thomas"

Table of Contents: List subtopics and page numbers, i.e.

Topic	Page
Introduction	1
The Battle of Bulldogs	2
The Veterinarian Strikes	3
(and so on)	

Paper organization:

Introductory paragraph(s)
Supportive paragraphs
Concluding or summary paragraph(s)
Appendices

Appendices: Appendices will include "Footnotes," "Bibliography," and any charts, maps, or graphs that support the topic.

Special Note: Researching should be fun. It is a literary adventure, much like Kojak or Columbo investigating a case, or Magic Johnson determining strategy against a basketball opponent.

Good luck. . . .

Cultural Awareness Module — English 101

Using a Library for Research

A library—college, university, or public—is a researcher's best friend. The more specific a researcher is regarding a topic, the easier it is to locate useful material. The following library resources are recommended.

A. Encyclopedias—Encyclopedias provide broad, general information about a topic and list more specific references. Encyclopedias also suggest related topics to explore. There are various types of encyclopedias; some are subject-oriented, while others are about geographical regions or specific fields of study.

B. The Card Catalog—The card catalog lists book subjects, titles, and authors held by the particular library.

C. Computer Searches—Many libraries provide the opportunity to search for information on a topic, author, or title from among one or more computer databases, as well as summarizing sources.

D. *Readers' Guide to Periodical Literature*—The *Readers' Guide* is a most useful resource that lists, by subject, magazine, special newspaper features, and journal articles.

E. Newspapers—Newspaper records can be used for information about events that occurred on or around certain dates. Newspapers are primarily viewed by researchers as secondary sources since information is quoted from or originated in another source.

F. Atlases and Maps—Atlases and maps are good places to start in learning about the major cities, geography, and location of a country, as well as about its topography, environment, and potential strategic concerns.

G. The Reference Librarian—A library's reference librarian is usually a knowledgeable, specially trained professional who can identify resources, in addition to those suggested above, that a particular library owns or has access to.

Sample Reference Card

_____   _____
subject   author

_____   _____
article topic   name of book or periodical

_____   _____
publisher   date of publication

Provide direct quotes "____" from resource or summary information and list page numbers

8

Using Reading Selections

The reading selections are nicely varied, interesting, and at an appropriate level of difficulty as well. I am particularly pleased with the gender/ethnic/topic balance.

Meredith A. Wilson, Solano Community College, CA

The reading selections are excellent in both their interest level and the strategies they illustrate.

Muriel Brennan, College of San Marco, CA

From Keysha Ingram-Gamor, Montgomery College, MD

Using Narration, Description, Illustration, Process, and Comparison and Contrast in Developmental English

RATIONALE

In developmental classes, I find it particularly useful for the students to see that what they read is current and pertinent to the world around them. In addition, I structure the individual writing assignments to ultimately evolve into a full multiparagraph essay. Each paragraph represents a stage in the development of the final paper. In an effort to evidence relevancy and continuity, I seek out additional reading material that the authors in *Evergreen* are publishing or material about the authors themselves. Students respond well to this approach, with relevant, thoughtful, and personal dialogue and writing.

One essay to which students respond well is Brent Staples's "A Brother's Murder." Among other pedagogical objectives and in an effort to encourage outside reading, I found excerpts about other pieces he's written. I use "Between Two Worlds," an article that features Staples's latest book, from *Time* magazine (March 7, 1994), to establish currency and relevancy. Since students can often relate in one way or another to the feelings of loss as well as to the feelings of hopelessness, guilt, frustration, and utter desperation that Staples expresses in "A Brother's Murder," they respond well to "Between Two Worlds," which offers additional insight into the environment that destroys Blake and eats away at Brent himself. Students are particularly intrigued by this article for many reasons, not the least of which is the other author featured in "Between Two Worlds." For these students, it is especially interesting that these destructive phenomena are not isolated incidences—rather, they are bewildering facts that shed some light on the world from which some hide and others try to escape. Most effective is the fact that we always have those students who can take us further into this "netherworld" for further examination and others who can inquire and study in order to respond more effectively to the diverse experiences around them. In either case, we all come away with mixed feelings of the "high" we get from learning something new, and the desperation we feel when there's something that seems out of our immediate control.

To broaden the scope further, I focus on these themes of hopelessness, guilt, frustration, responsibility, and utter desperation as we tiptoe toward another alarming world, very similar to that of Blake and Brent. Students are often wondering what went wrong, in Blake's world, that didn't doom Brent to the same sentiments and consequential fate. Many students related to the portrait of Blake as out of control, in search of a final resting place, racing toward the unknown with blind speed. Enabled to see that Blake could have been anyone within that given set of circumstances or something similar, students are empowered to read and respond more critically in their discourse. "Between Two

Worlds" provides students the opportunity to get a glimpse into the real issues that faced Brent and Blake, not only from Brent again but also from Nathan McCall.

At this juncture, I refer to some excerpts from McCall's *Makes Me Wanna Holler,* a book reviewed by Henry Louis Gates, Jr., and featured in The *New Yorker* under the title "Bad Influence." This series of reading material continues dialogue on many great themes, such as identity versus identification, finding a voice, family, relationships, determinism, victimization, realism, and so on. Since students generally respond so well to the text in *Evergreen* and are so involved in discussion, they really are able to grasp some more sophisticated literary terms and themes by examining these excerpts and articles. Interestingly enough, they remember this reading experience, and they are able to connect this experience with other readings as well as with their own experiences. All of a sudden, the students are reading for more than just an understanding of the plot. They begin to ask questions and share perceptions in ways they were incapable of before; furthermore, they are gaining confidence in their own interpretive abilities. Sharing new, in-depth insight is particularly exciting to students and me alike, for it truly takes their writing to a level they never thought they could get to.

SAMPLE WRITING ASSIGNMENTS *(Separate due dates for each assignment)*

1. Write about a time when you felt out of control. Describe only the event and your feelings. Do not expand any further at this point, for we are using this assignment as an opportunity to sharpen skills of narration and description. Pick your details carefully, choosing only the most accurate portrayal of what you experienced.

   Length: One paragraph of five to eight sentences.

2. Recall paper #1, about a time when you felt out of control. Explain either the steps you took to regain control or the stages of your succumbing to this overwhelming force in your life. What was your *response* to this feeling of losing control? What strategy did you develop in an effort to overcome the obstacle(s) you wrote about in paper #1?

   Length: One paragraph of five to eight sentences.

3. Write a paper in which you detail the response Blake (or Brent) had to his life-changing events. What did he do as he found himself in bad situations? Be sure to list as many examples as you can find in the text, "A Brother's Murder."

   Reminder: Be sure to record the page number of each example you extract from the text.

   Length: One paragraph of five to eight sentences.

4. Reflect on the similarities and/or differences between how you and Blake (or Brent), characters from "A Brother's Murder," respond to negative scenarios. Choose to discuss similarities or differences. (If you prefer, you may use the experiences of another author read in this course this semester.) Remember, this assignment calls for only one paragraph, so you will not have an opportunity to cover everything you might like.

   Suggestion: Write an informal outline in which you observe the characteristics of each person, and then choose which one you will use in your paper. I will collect the plans as well as the final paper.

   Length: One paragraph of five to eight sentences.

5. Write a multi-paragraph essay in which you discuss the following topic: *Responding to Negative Experiences.*

   Required materials: (There will be separate due dates for each stage of development.)

   - *Prewriting:* I will ask to see how you limited this topic to something specific; that is, your thesis statement.
   - *Organizing:* I will check for a formal outline for this paper.
   - *Revising and Editing:* I will look for an introduction, a conclusion, and a peer evaluation.
   - *Connecting:* I will expect you to include references to at least three relevant readings used in class so far, as well as your experiences developed in the previous paragraphs.

   Length: Three to five hundred words.

From Patricia Malinowski, Finger Lakes Community College, NY

Readings

Current literature reinforces the idea of the positive effect reading and writing have upon each other. I would strongly suggest that reading be incorporated in the course. The readings from the text should be assigned as part of class-discussion chapters or as part of the lecture component.

Sources include:

Congressional Digest—Monthly issues are devoted to one controversial congressional topic; pro and con arguments are presented by various U.S. representatives, senators, and special interest groups.

Editorials on File—A bimonthly newspaper editorial survey with a cumulative index.

Newsweek—Particularly the "My Turn" essays.

Social Issues Resources Series (SIRS)—Social and physical sciences; topical listing of articles from a large number of sources.

Time

USA Today—Particularly the editorial section, which often offers opposing viewpoints on a topic.

From Suzanne Doonan, Pennsylvania Institute of Technology, PA

English 100:
Selections to Read Aloud for Writing Prompts

"Learning to Write" by Russell Baker, in *Patterns Plus,* Houghton Mifflin, 1995
> Students describe a time in their lives when they realized that they had a special skill or talent.

"The Magic Pebbles" from *A 2nd Helping of Chicken Soup for the Soul*
> Students describe an experience or a person who seemed like a "pebble" but later became a "diamond" in their lives.

Selections from the following books:

Chicken Soup for the Soul by Mark Canfield and Victor Hansen, Health Communications, Inc., Deerfield, FL, 1995

Random Acts of Kindness and *More Random Acts of Kindness* by The Editors of Conari Press, 1993
> Students respond by relating personal experiences or the actions of others that have made a lasting impression on them.

The Book of Questions by Gregory Stock, Workman Publishing, 1987
> Questions such as "Given the choice of anyone in the world, whom would you want as your dinner guest? (page 48)

> Some questions work well for dialogue journals. Students write a 3–5 sentence response and pass the paper to another student. Papers are passed among 4–5 students.

Politically Correct Bedtime Stories by James Finn Garner, MacMillan, 1994

From Sandra K. Hall, Corning Community College, CA

Using Readings with *Evergreen*

1. Find a sentence in the *factual article* attached from a reputable newspaper or weekly magazine (such as *Time*) that also includes a **colorful description** or uses an effective **active verb.**

2. Quote the sentence you have selected by writing it word-for-word in section #3 of this handout. Be sure to use **quotation marks.**

3. On the photocopy, highlight or <u>underline</u> the sentence you have quoted.

4. **Work Cited:** Include the bibliographic information in the order indicated (MLA style).

5. You must follow *all* directions to receive a grade.

Example from a *weekly* magazine:

#2: Quote:

"As the bonfire crackles, the campers sit around in a circle and roast marshmallows and giggle."

#4:   Work Cited

Gordon, Jeanne. "No Pampers, Pampering: A Cushy Camp for Moms." <u>Newsweek</u> 10 July 1989: 76.

Example from a *Newspaper:* (no author provided)

#2: Quote:

"Inside a cluster of plush buildings baked by the Silicon Valley sun, Apple Computer Inc. employees wearing sport shirts and jeans are readying products they hope will revive the company's breathtaking growth."

#4:   Work Cited

"Apple's Future Clouded by Stepped-up Competition." <u>Star Gazette</u> 17 July 1990: 1D.

Your Selection:

- Highlight your selected sentence.
- Copy the sentence you've selected, exactly as it appears in the article.
- BE SURE TO USE QUOTATION MARKS AT THE BEGINNING AND END of your quote.

#2: My Quote:

_____

_____

_____

_____

_____

_____

_____

_____

#4   Work Cited

_____, _____ . _____
(Author's last name),   (First Name).   (Put title of article in quotation

_____ . _____
marks & capitalize.)   (Title of magazine or paper, underlined)

_____ .
(Date   Month   Year) **:** (Complete pages of article).

Make sure you follow this pattern for citing the article:

EXAMPLE: Work Cited

Gordon, Jeanne. "No Pampers, Pampering: A Cushy Camp for Moms."
    Newsweek 10 July 1989: 76.

From Ann L. Lathrop, Lehman College, NY

Some Notes on Writing and Reading
with *Evergreen*

Required Texts and Supplies

Evergreen with Readings by Fawcett and Sandberg, 5th Edition

Bless Me, Ultima by Rudolfo Anaya (TQS Publications, Berkeley, CA)

An English dictionary with at least 50,000 entries: *Longman Dictionary of Contemporary English, New Edition* (highly recommended)

A looseleaf notebook with 8½ x 11" paper (no spiral fringes, please) in which *all* the semester's work—notes, brainstorming, drafts, revisions, and Reader Responses—is kept.

Looseleaf section dividers

Index cards

Other Required Works

Genesis 1–3, King James Version

"Childhood and the Garden of Eden" by Marie Winn (Full publishing information follows.)

"Young Goodman Brown" by Nathaniel Hawthorne

Stand by Me, film available on videotape

I have used *Evergreen* successfully with lower and upper intermediate/lower advanced ESL classes in college developmental English programs. In the more advanced classes, the emphasis is on writing essays, especially persuasive ones, as students must show minimum competence in written English based on a 50-minute essay examination (the CUNY Writing Assessment Tests) with essay prompts that state a position and ask students to agree or disagree with that statement. I have found it helpful to expand some of the treatment of grammatical structures presented in *Evergreen,* because of the needs of ESL students and to have the more advanced classes write paragraphs closely related to the book(s) that they are reading for the course, to practice rhetorical modes and and then to extend the scope of their writing to full essays, using several of the modes as arguments to support a general thesis.

For example, when the class was reading *Bless Me, Ultima* by Rudolfo Anaya, a paragraph describing Ultima exercised present tense subject-verb agreement and followed the **descriptive** mode. Similarly, paragraphs **comparing and contrasting** the golden carp and the black bass, and Narciso's garden with the Garden of Eden, correlated well with Chapter 10. Work later in the semester called upon the students to compare and contrast the themes and features of *Bless Me, Ultima* and the film *Stand by Me:*

> Stories about boys growing up may be separated by culture and other factors, but they may still have many themes and features in common. In what ways were *Bless Me, Ultima* and *Stand by Me* similar and in what ways were they different? Using specific examples from both the book and the film, compare and contrast these two works in a well-organized, well-edited essay.

In another instance, students used the modals (*would, could,* etc.), extending the work of Chapter 25 in a paragraph in the **process** mode to explain how they would train a *curandera/o* (herbalist), using Ultima's behavior toward Antonio as a guide. A later essay in the **persuasive** mode that worked well explored whether the student believed that such a person or such knowledge was applicable in current daily life:

> "Ultima was a curandera, a woman who knew the herbs and remedies of the ancients, a miracle-worker who could heal the sick" (Anaya 4). At the same time, some people feared her and thought that she was a witch. Why might people have this opinion of such a person? Do you think that there is a place for this type of healer in our scientifically advanced society? Would you ever consult a person like her or advise someone else to do so? Why or why not?

Another such assignment that elicited good writing was one that called upon knowledge of the book and drew upon personal experience and observations, and for which students were guided to use the modes of **cause and effect, process, and illustration** to discuss parental direction in career choice:

> Parents know their children's strengths and weaknesses better than anyone else, and they are familiar with the world into which their children are growing. Therefore, they should be the ones to decide their children's professions.
>
> Do you agree or disagree? Using the following essay elements, explain and illustrate your answer, drawing upon your own experience, your observation of others, and your reading.
>
> 1. An **introductory** paragraph that states your position.
> 2. A paragraph that supports your thesis by predicting the **consequence.**
> 3. A paragraph that includes **reference** to *Bless Me, Ultima* and an **illustration** from your own observation or experience to support your position.
> 4. A well-developed **process** paragraph that supports your thesis and that tells how a career should be selected.
> 5. A **concluding** paragraph that sums up your essay and gives the reader something interesting to think about.

Along with the theme of friendship, the theme of coming of age or the loss of innocence is of interest to college students, and my more advanced students respond well to Genesis 1–3, read as background for Marie Winn's essay "Childhood and the Garden of Eden" (reprinted in *Purpose and Process* by Jeffrey D. Hoeper and James H. Pickering, New York: Macmillan, reprinted from *Children without Childhood,* Pantheon Books/Random House) and Nathaniel Hawthorne's "Young Goodman Brown." These pieces of writing are mind-stretching and linguistically challenging for the most developmental and ESL English students and give a taste of the level of reading expected in college work. Thorough in-class discussion after students have read the pieces on their own can lead to a sense of mastery of and confidence in dealing with the material as well as pleasure in dealing with the ideas. Winn's essay also lends itself to a lesson in outlining and summary, necessary skills for college students.

Reading and Reader Response Schedule
for
Bless Me, Ultima

Day	Date	Chapter(s) BMU	Pages BMU	Reader Response	Grammar/Wri. *Evergreen* Chap.
Tuesday	Feb. 1				Parts of Speech
Friday	Feb. 4	1, 2	1–23		1, 2 (pp. 2–7)
Tuesday	Feb. 8	3, 4	25–43	I	Sentence Functions 21
Friday	Feb.11	College Closed–Lincoln's Birthday			
Tuesday	Feb. 15	5–9	44–75	II	3, 5
Friday	Feb. 18	10	76–97		22
Tuesday	Feb. 22	11	98–113	III	6
Friday	Feb. 25	12, 13	114–136		23, 7
Tuesday	Mar. 1	14	137–168	IV	8
Friday	Mar. 4	15, 16	169–182		24, 10
Tuesday	Mar. 8	17, 18	183–194	V	12
Friday	Mar. 11	19, 20	207–225		25
Tuesday	Mar. 15	21, 22	226–248	VI	
Friday	Mar. 18	Midsemester Exam			26
Tuesday	Mar. 22				27
Friday	Mar. 25	Library Session			

─────────────────── **SPRING VACATION** ───────────────────

Day	Date	Chapter(s) BMU	Pages BMU	Reader Response	Grammar/Wri. *Evergreen* Chap.
Tuesday	Apr. 5				29
Friday	Apr. 8				
Tuesday	Apr. 12				30
Friday	Apr. 15				
Tuesday	Apr. 19				31
Friday	Apr. 22				
Tuesday	Apr. 26				32
Friday	Apr. 29				33
Tuesday	May 3				
Friday	May 6	Department Final—Essay			
Tuesday	May 10	WAT (Program Exit Exam) CELT (Grammar Proficiency Exam)			

9

Writing
with
Computers

As an instructor you can *intervene* in the writing process more quickly and easily in a computer lab than in the traditional classroom, thus making your teaching more effective. You can read what students write on the screen over their shoulders, so to speak, without the cumbersome interruption that would be necessary in picking up manuscript pages. You're like a swimming coach who can watch students in the water and correct problems at once.

George Moberg, Borough of Manhattan Community College, City University of New York, NY

From Patricia Malinowski, Finger Lakes Community College, NY

Computer Component

Computer usage has been integrated into College Composition as an important component of the course. Student computer use is strongly encouraged. Current literature, although inconclusive at this point, does offer strong arguments for computer use with developmental students and has shown positive effects on student writing in this course.

The art of revising and editing is important and can be easily accomplished upon the computer. As students become conversant with the computer, they often find that it becomes one of their most effective writing tools.

The instructor should schedule a class in the computer classroom early in the semester. Students will be taught computer use and either the *PFS Write* or the *WordPerfect* word processing program. Additional class time should be scheduled in the classroom throughout the semester.

More computer software is available for instructor review and use in the computer classroom. There are several grammar and writing programs that could be used to supplement instruction.

From Sandra K. Hall, Corning Community College, NY

Integrating Writing Activities
with Basic Computer Skills

I have designed my Basic Writing course to **integrate** the writing activities with basic computer skills and with grammar and mechanics as they are taught in the co-required grammar course. When we adopted *Evergreen*, I collaborated with my colleague Andrea Rubin, who teaches the one-credit grammar course. The focus of the writing course remains upon the writing process, not upon the wizardry of the computer or on grammar drills. Andrea Rubin and I continue our collaboration as we strengthen the link between Reading Skills and Basic Writing. *Evergreen with Readings* has been helpful with this endeavor. I begin the course with the following assignment sequence on descriptive writing.

Descriptive Writing

Week 1

During Week One, students have done a simple exercise on the computer and read Chapter 1, Part B, on "Subject, Audience, and Purpose," and Chapter 2, "Gathering Ideas." Then I introduce descriptive writing, which will be our focus for the next 3–4 weeks.

- We read p. 20, Practice l, paragraph *a;* Maya Angelou's description of a summer picnic, and identify the details that grab our senses—"spareribs *sputtered*" and "Pound cakes *sagged.*" The details are specific: it's *Hershey's* chocolate that is "dripping." Two qualities of descriptive writing become apparent: sensory details and active verbs. (Students will be working on parts of speech in their grammar module.)

- Next, we look at Chapter 3, p. 24, where we discuss "Pete's sloppiness." I have the students form six groups, and one student sits at the end computer of each row. (I ask for volunteers who don't mind typing.) Then each group brainstorms details to add to the topic. After about five minutes we stop and see which group has generated the best list, and we share some, and print our lists. (These are not collected.)

- Then I show the class on the syllabus, the topic for Journal 2: "Describe the current state of your desk, your car, your kitchen, or your closet." I add, "Be sure to have sensory details and active verbs. This is due on Monday."

Week 2

- We discuss what would make a unified paragraph on Pete's sloppiness. Then I have the students turn to Practice 10, p. 37, where we look at paragraph *a.* I ask them what sentence is the topic sentence and have them highlight that sentence in their text. (This is a practice we continue when we are reading in the text. When they have learned *bold* and *underline,* I show them how to use these commands in their drafts.) Then we look for a sentence that does not fit, discuss why it doesn't, and cross it out.

- At this point, we take our books to the computers and open a file I've created called "Unity." I have simply keyed in paragraphs *a, b,* and *c* of Practice 10. I then show students how to *delete* the offending sentence in *a.* On their own, they delete a sentence in (*b*). They struggle with (*c*) because the topic sentence is the problem. Together, we delete the topic sentence and type in an appropriate one. We save the changes we've made, but I do not collect this. What I do stress, however, is not just the computer skill of "delete," but the importance of looking at a text with a critical eye in order to delete something that hurts the unity of a paragraph.

- I ask them to find in their notebook a handout Linda Perry (Assistant Director of our Communications Learning Center) helped me create, titled "Building Blocks to Effective Persuasive Writing." We created this handout to provide a visualization of the key Methods of Persuasion *Evergreen* outlines on pp.150–151. Students, even at the end of the term, often have trouble grasping the value of these pages, but I feel these "blocks" are used in varying degrees by good writers to build the foundation of their paragraphs or essays. I tell the class that the handout will be used throughout the semester and that eventually, its importance will be clear. What we are interested in right now is an essential building block that each writer uses—facts—and details. (However, it is also important for students to see that there is a "big picture" and all of our work is building toward an ultimate goal.)

- Next I distribute to each student an interesting photograph from my collection. I tell them they have five minutes to get on a piece of paper enough of the specific details of the photo that someone else in the class could easily find it. I then collect the photos, arrange them randomly on the table, and have students each exchange lists with someone across the room. Each student reads the list, then searches for the correct photo. (I throw in several photos of unidentifiable magnifications of fungi and mold, to make some harder to distinguish from others!) Students have fun with this simple activity. I like it because it engages several of the Seven Intelligences—visual, verbal, interpersonal, and kinesthetic—and because it demonstrates the reality of audience. We discuss what details were helpful and what were not.

- Together, we look at paragraph 3 at the top of page 57. We identify the active verbs that make the paragraph effective: "clicks," "flops," "stares," and "whimper."

- Next, students open a file called "Active" in which I have typed a relatively uninteresting paragraph describing the line and the process for getting your books during the first week of classes. The boring verbs are in **boldface.** I show how easy it is to replace a weak verb with an active one, and how dramatically it helps the paragraph come to life.

- Students complete a Planning Sheet for Paragraph 1 that asks them to brainstorm and organize details: "Describe in detail an object in your junk drawer, desk, or tool box. You will not name this object in your paragraph. On Peer Review day, you will bring your rough draft *and* the object to class."

Handout:
Building Blocks to Effective
Persuasive Writing

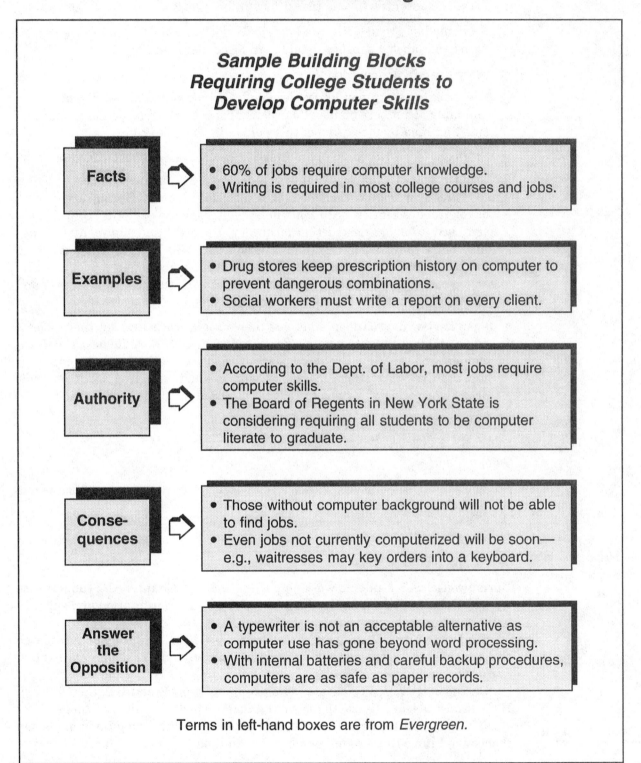

Sample Building Blocks
Requiring College Students to
Develop Computer Skills

Facts
- 60% of jobs require computer knowledge.
- Writing is required in most college courses and jobs.

Examples
- Drug stores keep prescription history on computer to prevent dangerous combinations.
- Social workers must write a report on every client.

Authority
- According to the Dept. of Labor, most jobs require computer skills.
- The Board of Regents in New York State is considering requiring all students to be computer literate to graduate.

Conse-quences
- Those without computer background will not be able to find jobs.
- Even jobs not currently computerized will be soon—e.g., waitresses may key orders into a keyboard.

Answer the Opposition
- A typewriter is not an acceptable alternative as computer use has gone beyond word processing.
- With internal batteries and careful backup procedures, computers are as safe as paper records.

Terms in left-hand boxes are from *Evergreen*.

Week 3

- We read the paragraph on King Tut's tomb in Chapter 7, p. 87. We highlight the topic sentence, circle descriptive details, and underline transitions. Here students begin to see the function of transitions. They also open a file called "Transit" and insert some transitions in bold.

- Students have read "Disney's Perfect World," on 277–278 and circled active verbs and labeled sensory details. We discuss this essay.

- They hand in Journal 3:

  "Describe a person you know very well. Include physical details, behavior, and hints about personality. Your journal sheet will be sealed in a time capsule and read by a relative of this person in the year 2050."

- Students begin Research l, the first of twelve research assignments:

  "Find a sentence in a factual article in a weekly magazine such as *Time, Newsweek,* or *Sports Illustrated* that also contains an effective active verb or colorful description." Students must photocopy the page that contains the sentence (to avoid destruction of library property) and highlight it. They also must provide bibliographic information. This assignment gets them to the library, illustrates that published writers use effective details and active verbs, and begins to familiarize them with the research process and MLA style. They have a week to complete this.

- Peer Review day: Students get out their rough drafts and set their objects on the table. Students who are prepared, receive a Peer Review sheet, exchange with another prepared person, read each other's work, and offer constructive suggestions. Students who are not prepared work on their drafts and forfeit the right to rewrite the final draft for a new grade.

- Final draft is due at the end of this week.

Weeks 4 and 5

Students repeat the process with a second descriptive paragraph, which is due the first class of Week 5.

Process Writing

During weeks 5–7, students work on process writing (Chapter 8). Students also work in Chapter 22 on using conjunctive adverbs and coordination and subordination, in the grammar course.

Students write a journal entry in the process mode, and they do a research assignment that involves group work on finding an address of an organization in the library Reference Room.

On the computer, I've entered two examples from Practice 2, pp. 103–105. Here, students learn to use the *move* command where it really matters—to get steps in the correct order. We walk through #1: how chewing gum is made. On their own, I have them complete another example.

Tips on Using the Computer
to Improve Your Writing

Together, there are many "tricks" we can develop to help you improve your own writing.

Step 1: Get comfortable using the computer.

Step 2: Take the Prewriting (Brainstorming) stage and the Rough Draft stage seriously.

Step 3: Save periodically—at least every *15* minutes. Use F10 key.

NOTE: Writings can be named and renamed:

Cars.1	prewriting about cars owned
Cars.2	rough draft
Cars.3	final draft

Sample assignment: Write a well-developed paragraph showing *examples* of cars.

Rough Draft stage: Remember, you can put any notes, etc, in this stage that you want to—because these can easily be removed for the final draft.

1. Topic sentence:

   a. topic   +   attitude:

   All the *cars* I have bought have been *lemons.*

   ---

   b. Get into the habit of <u>underlining</u> your topic sentence.

   (This reminds you to focus on this important, controlling sentence.)

2. Leave yourself notes—if you are stuck on a word, or its spelling, or not sure you are happy with a sentence or a paragraph, write yourself a few ??????? and come back to it.

Have you saved recently?   **F10 key**

---

3. Look back at your underlined topic sentence—are you providing information, evidence, details to help the reader follow your point? If not, revise.

4. Are your ideas, examples, details in the best order? If not, ask for help to use the *move* command to fix the order without retyping.

5. Are your examples as **specific** as possible? Do you say:

> All the cars I have bought—from the Jeep to the Pinto to the Volkswagen—have been lemons.

or

> All the cars I have bought have been lemons. The Jeep came with a transmission that was always breaking down. The Pinto was rusting the day I drove it out of the lot. The Volkswagen cost a lot of money, but it still was in the garage every month to have the heater, horn, speedometer, or brakes fixed.

6. Have I used transitions to help my reader get from idea to idea?

> All the cars I have bought have been lemons. First, my Jeep came with a transmission that was always breaking down. My next car, a Pinto, was rusting the day I drove it out of the lot. Finally, my Volkswagen cost a lot of money, but it still was in the garage every month to have the heater, horn, speedometer, or brakes fixed.

7. Does my paragraph have a **summary sentence**—or does it leave the reader "hanging"?

> All the cars I have bought have been lemons. First, my Jeep came with a transmission that was always breaking down. My next car, a Pinto, was rusting the day I drove it out of the lot. Finally, my Volkswagen cost a lot of money, but it still was in the garage every month to have the heater, horn, speedometer, or brakes fixed. When I buy my next car, I am going to read all the consumer reports on it before I buy it!

8. Do you tend to have FRAGMENTS, COMMA SPLICES, or RUN-ONS?

    √ Save a version of your paper by labeling it. **Hobby.sen.**
      (This will tell you that you saved a version of a writing on a hobby and checked if for sentence problems.)
    √ Then put your cursor after each period, so that sentences occupy their own set of lines.

✓ Next, examine each line.
- Very short ones may be fragments.
- Long ones may be comma splices or fragments.
- Many short sentences may indicate a short, choppy style.
- Use this "MAP" of your sentence length to decide how to
    1. combine ideas for clarity and variety.
    2. add transitions to help your reader follow.

Have you saved recently?   **F10 key**

Final Draft:

1. Have you **proofread** your final draft several times—line-by-line or even from bottom to top?

2. Remember to use a SPELLCHECKER to help yourself find most spelling errors.

CTRLF2 key

3. If you find yourself using one word over and over, use the thesaurus on the computer to find other words.

4. Have your checked your **Peer Review?**

5. Have you checked your draft for weaknesses you listed on your Writing Strengths and Weaknesses form?

6. Should some of these short sentences be combined to make your writing less choppy and to show how ideas are connected?

choppy:

| My first car was a Jeep. I bought it in 1985. |
| It had problems with its transmission from day one. |

better:

| In 1985, I was disappointed in my first car, a Jeep, |
| because the transmission was always breaking down. |

7. Is it overly long?

Maybe you are being wordy. Have the courage to cut out unneeded words.

8. Does each sentence begin the same way?

   I did this. Then I did that. (etc.)—Revise.

Have you saved recently?   **F10 key**

Publish: Print out your final draft.

1. Create a title page that has a clear and interesting title.

   > *Cars*

   or

   > ***Lemons I Have Owned!***

2. Include everything—in your folder for formal writings. Make sure that your **title page** and **final draft** are the *first* things I see inside the folder.

3. REMEMBER: Late papers *cannot be rewritten*. Being late with final drafts cancels your rewrite option.

4. Remember, grades are lowered for

   > lateness,
   > careless errors like "alot" for "a lot," and
   > incomplete Peer Review sheets.

Moving from Paragraph to Essay

Remember our paragraph on cars?

> All the cars I have bought have been lemons. First, my Jeep came with a transmission that was always breaking down. My next car, a Pinto, was rusting the day I drove it out of the lot. Finally, my Volkswagen cost a lot of money, but it still was in the garage every month to have the heater, horn, speedometer, or brakes fixed. When I buy my next car, I am going to read all the consumer reports on it before I buy it!

Let's expand it to an essay:

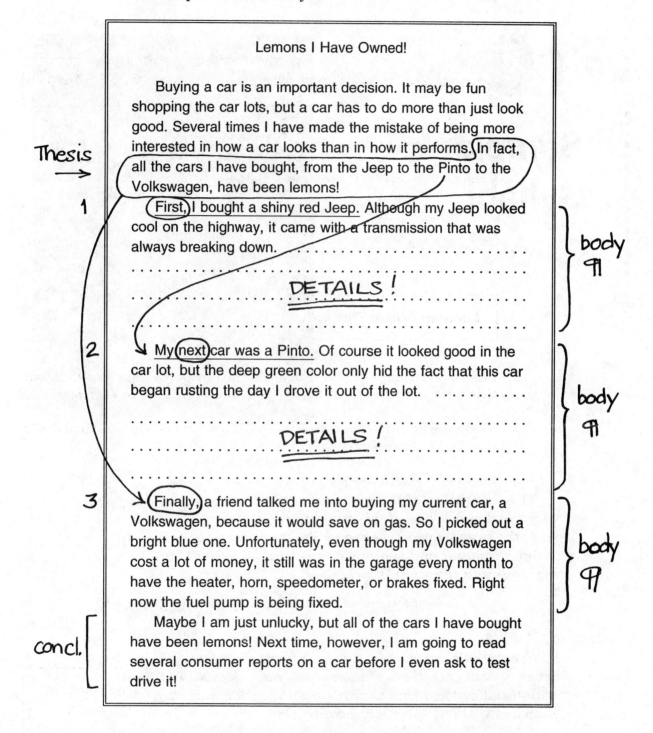

Thesis →

Lemons I Have Owned!

Buying a car is an important decision. It may be fun shopping the car lots, but a car has to do more than just look good. Several times I have made the mistake of being more interested in how a car looks than in how it performs. In fact, all the cars I have bought, from the Jeep to the Pinto to the Volkswagen, have been lemons!

1   First, I bought a shiny red Jeep. Although my Jeep looked cool on the highway, it came with a transmission that was always breaking down.

DETAILS !

body ¶

2   My next car was a Pinto. Of course it looked good in the car lot, but the deep green color only hid the fact that this car began rusting the day I drove it out of the lot.

DETAILS !

body ¶

3   Finally, a friend talked me into buying my current car, a Volkswagen, because it would save on gas. So I picked out a bright blue one. Unfortunately, even though my Volkswagen cost a lot of money, it still was in the garage every month to have the heater, horn, speedometer, or brakes fixed. Right now the fuel pump is being fixed.

body ¶

concl.   Maybe I am just unlucky, but all of the cars I have bought have been lemons! Next time, however, I am going to read several consumer reports on a car before I even ask to test drive it!

10

Sample Syllabi

The separation of the grammar and writing sections is very good and is one of the advantages of using *Evergreen*. With the organization the way it is, the instructor is free to assign grammar and sentence structure along with the readings and the writing practices.

Debra Anderson, Indian River Community College, FL

Evergreen's units logically classify all the appropriate areas of concentration. Though I seldom assign the units in sequential order, I find that it's easy to mix and match chapters without sacrificing continuity.

Debra Callen, Harold Washington College, IL

From Keysha Ingram-Gamor, Montgomery College, MD

Course Syllabus

Welcome to English 001, Basic English. This course will serve as a review of basic principles of English usage including fundamentals of sentence patterns, simple grammar, elementary punctuation, mechanics, and an introduction to the writing of short paragraphs and brief essays. English 001 is a five-hour non-credit course. Upon completion of this course, students will be evaluated for progression into credit English courses.

In addition to the requirements on the other handouts you have received, this one is vital to your success in this course. Please keep it, along with the other handouts, in your three-ring binder, as you will need to refer to all of these documents often.

Required Texts

Fawcett, Susan. *Evergreen.* Fifth Edition. Houghton Mifflin, 1996. **AND**
Selby, Norwood. *Essential College English.* Third Edition. HarperCollins
  Publishers, 1991.

Oral Reports / Written Reports

Each student is required to read one novel for this course. Choose from the collection of excerpts from novels in the Reading section of the Tutoring Center in Humanities 21.

You must submit a one-page summary for *each set of two to three chapters as you read the book; **otherwise, your final presentation will not be accepted***. These summaries should be handed in every Friday until your novel is completed. You may use audiovisual material to aid your 10–15 minute presentation.

Give a brief biography about the author.

List some other popular books written by the author.

Explain why you chose this book.

Describe what you liked best about this book.

Tell how reading this book has enhanced your academic or personal life.

Detail whether or not you'd recommend this book and why or why not.

Add any other pertinent information (e.g., music, pictures, recipes, clothes, documents, or whatever else from that period).

The oral portion of this project is optional; however, giving the presentation will earn you extra credit. The extra credit may be applied to any grade category.

Grade Categories

Class participation (includes all class assignments, use of class time, and class discussions), homework, quizzes, tests, papers, formal report, computer room assignments, Tutoring Center assignments, MC Composition folder, and department exams.

English 001 Montgomery College Composition Folder
CHECKLIST
Prof. K. Gamor
Fall 1995

Since all folders must be in good order before they are considered for evaluation, I have made a checklist to help you stay organized. I hope that you will find this useful. Upon your final evaluation on December 15, 1995, you shall be required to include this as the final sheet in your folder. If you have any questions, please don't hesitate to schedule a conference.

All items listed below should appear in reverse chronological order in your MC Composition folder. The items that you will have in your folder are as follows:

_____ **Diagnostic Writing Assignment 9/6**—Score: _____

_____ **Diagnostic Sentence Skills Test 9/6**—Score: _____

_____   Illustration Paragraph (p. 76 *Evergreen*)

_____   Narration Paragraph (p. 85 *Evergreen*)

_____   Description Paragraph (Assignment Sheet)

_____ Midterm Writing Exam—Score: _____

_____ Midterm Sentence Skills Exam—Score: _____

_____   Process How-to—in-class writing (Assignment Sheet)

_____   Process Explanation—in-class writing (Assignment Sheet)

_____   Comparison & Contrast—multiparag.

_____   Definition & Classification—multiparag.

_____ Grammar Review Sheets (2 sheets per topic)

_____   1. Subject, Verb, Complement

2. Topic Sentences

3. Sentence Variety

4. Consistency and Parallelism

5. Commas

6. Comma Splice & Fused Sentences

7. Apostrophes

8. Active & Passive Voice

9. Homophones

10. Independent Study Sheets

_____   Tutoring Assignment Packet

_____   Mandatory Biweekly Conferences

_____ Final Writing Exam: Score: _____

_____ Final Sentence Skills Exam: Score: _____

_____ MC Composition Final Folder

Course Schedule

Expect a quiz weekly.

September

W	9/6	Diagnostic Test Series
F	9/8	Diagnostic Test Series
	HW:	Due Monday: Read pp. 2–41 in *Evergreen*

M	9/11	In-class: Coherence and Topic Sentences
		Homework: Read and do *ECE* pp. 3–15—Due 9/13
W	9/13	In-class: Complements *ECE* pp. 17–24
		Homework: Reading *Evergreen* pp. 489–492 "A Brother's Murder"
F	9/15	In-class: Round table discussion
		Homework: Read and do pp. 35–60 in *ECE*

M	9/18	In-class: pp. 387–391, 394–405, 414–420 in *Evergreen*
		Homework: pp.410–413 *Evergreen* (Prepositions)
W	9/20	In-class: *ECE* pp. 81–95; pp. 78–96 *Evergreen*
		Homework: Read pp. 480–486 *Evergreen*
F	9/22	In-class: Round table discussion
		Homework: Description Assignment Sheet

M	9/25	*Review for Unit Test*
W	9/27	*Unit Test: Topic Sent., Subj., Verb, Complement, Parts of Speech*
F	9/29	*Computer Room: Skills Bank*
		Homework: Read pp. 98–107 *Evergreen*

October

M	10/2	In-class: Reading pp. 98–107 *Evergreen* Writing: Process
W	10/4	In-class writing: Process
F	10/6	Comma Splices and Fused Sentences
		Homework: Read and do pp. 267–271 *ECE*

M	10/9	In-class: Comma workshop
		Homework: Read and do pp. 189–195 *ECE*
W	10/11	In-class: Sentence Fragments and Run-on Sentences
F	10/13	In-class: Sentence Variety
		Homework: Deluxe Pizza

M	10/16	In-class: Sentence Types pp. 123 *ECE*
		Homework: Come to class with questions about test material.
W	10/18	*Computer Room: Skills Bank* / Review Day for Unit Test
F	10/20	Unit Test: Commas, Comma Splices, Fused Sentences, Sentence Fragments, Sentence Variety
		Homework: Read and do pp. 164–169 *Evergreen*

M	10/23	In-class: pp. 169–180 *Evergreen*
W	10/25	In-class: pp. 218–228 *Evergreen*
F	10/27	**Midterm**

November

M	10/30	Learning to Revise: A Workshop
W	11/1	Learning to Revise: A Workshop
F	11/3	*Computer Room: Skills Bank* Read pp. 242–243 *Evergreen*

M	11/6	In-class: pp. 239–263 *Evergreen*
W	11/8	In-class: pp. 291–296 *Evergreen*
F	11/10	In-class: p. 300–315 *Evergreen* Homework: Read and do pp. 120–137 *Evergreen*

M	11/13	In-class: Read pp. 492–496 *Evergreen*
W	11/15	In-class: Read pp. 283–285 *Evergreen*
F	11/17	*Multiparagraph Assignment*

M	11/20	*Writing*
W	11/22	Computer Room: Skills Bank
F	11/24	**No Class—College Closed for Thanksgiving Holiday**

M	11/27	**Multiparagraph Essay Due** **Oral Reports/Formal Reports Due**
W	11/29	Apostrophe
F	12/1	Mechanics

December

M	12/4	Look-Alikes/Sound-Alikes
W	12/6	Read pp. 108–119 *Evergreen* Homework: Complete Exercises
F	12/8	Read pp. 138–146 *Evergreen*

M	12/11	Assignment Sheet: Definition & Classification—At end of period DUE: Prewriting
W	12/13	In-class drafting
F	12/15	Multiparagraph Essay: Definition & Classification Due

M	12/18	**Week of Exams at Montgomery College**
W	12/20	*Your exam will be this week; you will be informed of the day when*
F	12/22	*I receive the schedule. Our class will not meet on the other days.*

Happy Holidays and Best Wishes for the New Year!

From Susan McKnight, Tarrant County Junior College, TX

Calendar for English 1203

Developmental English — Spring 1995

		Underlining indicates assignment due for that class.
TU	1/17	Introduction to course Writing sample Introduction to the writing process
TH	1/19	Evergreen Ch 1 + Ch 21 A–B Sentence — subjects, verbs Generating ideas: freewriting, brainstorming
TU	1/24	Prewriting for Paragraph #1 + Ch 2 A–B Generating ideas: clustering, webbing Writing process Sentence — coordination
TH N304	1/26 Writing Center	Ch2 C–D — Ch 22 A + Bring #262 Scantron and #2 pencil Orientation + take Diagnostic Test Draft and revise paragraph #1.
TU	1/31	Paragraph #1 + Ch 3 A–B (Odd) Sentence — coordination Narrowing and focusing topic: the topic sentence
TH	2/2	Ch 22 B + Ch 3 D–E–F Sentence — subordination Supporting the topic sentence = Prewriting Pgr. # 2
TU	2/7	Ch 22 B–C–D + read "How to Get the Most . . ." pp. 499–502 Other sentence patterns + correcting run-ons Supporting the topic sentence + draft Pgr. #2
TH	2/9	Paragraph #2 + Ch 22E + Ch 23 A Sentence — correcting fragments Paragraph — development and coherence
TU	2/14	Ch 23B + Ch 4A Note: test on Ch 21–23 next class Sentence — correcting run-ons and fragments + review Paragraph coherence = in-class revision of Pgr. #1 or #2

1203 Course Calendar			McKnight p. 2
		<u>Underlining indicates assignment due for that class.</u>	
TH	2/16	<u>Review Ch 21–22–23 for Test 1 + Ch 4B</u> TEST 1: <u>Evergreen</u> Ch 21–22–23 (green Scantron) Description: prewriting of Pgr. #3	
TU N304	2/21 Writing Center	<u>Rough copy Paragraph #3 (description) due + Ch 24, 25</u> Writing Center orientation Begin individual Writing Center assignments.	
TH N304	2/23 Writing Center	<u>Ch 25 and 26</u> Continue Writing Center assignments. Verbs	
TU N304	2/28 Writing Center	<u>Ch 7 pp. 81–86 (all) + Final copy Pgr. #3</u> Individual conferences Continue Writing Center assignments.	
TH	3/2	<u>Review Ch 24, 25, 28 + Pgr. #4 due (a revision of any previous pgr.)</u> Verbs + review of pgr. structure (3F) complete Wr. Center work	
TU	3/7	<u>Ch 12 + Ch 17A</u> Introduction to the essay outline Grammar review and spelling	
TH	3/9	<u>Ch 27, 28 + essay outline sheet</u> Nouns and pronouns + spelling review Start prewriting and essay outline (persuasive)	
TU/TH	3/14 & 3/16	**Spring Break — No class . . . . Catch up, review, relax**	
TU	3/21	<u>Essay Outline + Ch 29</u> Grammar: review + propositions and spelling Thesis statement	
TH	3/23	<u>Ch 17B–C + prewriting for essay #1</u> Grammar review for Ch 24–29 Begin outline for essay #1.	
TU	3/28	<u>Review Ch 24–29 for Test #2</u> Test #2: <u>Evergreen</u> Ch 24–29 (green Scantron) Rough copy of essay #1	
TH	3/30	<u>Ch 32A–C (odd) + bring outline essay #1</u> Peer revision of essay #1 + rewriting (essay due end of class) Spelling review + begin comma	

1203 Course Calendar		**McKnight p. 3**

TU	4/4
	
	Writing
	Center
		Ch 17 D, E + read "A Brother's Murder" pp. 489–492
		
		  Complete work in Writing Center (or practice for objective
		  part of TASP).

TH	4/6	Ch 19 A, B + Ch 32 D–F (odd)
		
		  Comma review
		  Review of intro. & Concl. + revision of essay #1

TU	4/11	Ch 32 review + Ch 33A
		
		  Workshop: writing the in-class essay
		  The comma

TH	4/13	Ch 18H + Read "Hunger of Memory" pp. 502–506 In-class writing of essay #2

TU	4/18
	
	Writing
	Center
		ALL WR. CENTER WORK DUE IN FOLDERS N304
		
		  Post Test for Wr. C enter assignments
		  (Bring pink Scantron #262)

TH	4/20	Ch 33 A + revision of Essay #2 In-class writing of essay #3

TU	4/25	Ch 33 B and D
		
		  Revision of essay 3
		  Mechanics

TH	4/27	Review essays
		
		  In-class PTT WRITING SAMPLE
		
		  NOTE: Final exam + RTT
		  You must complete both parts of PTT to receive 1203 credit.

TU	5/2	Review grammar sheets + Appendix #2
		
		  Review sentence and paragraph structure.
		  Spelling and commonly confused words
		  Review for PTT

TH	5/4 C-113	Meet in Testing Center for PTT MULTIPLE CHOICE TEST WRITING TEST
TU or TH	5/9 or 5/11	Final exam period — Meet in classroom during scheduled exam time for individual conference.

Course Outline

COURSE OBJECTIVE: Upon successful completion of this course the student will be expected to:

1. Demonstrate increased control of the writing process, evidenced by multi-paragraph writings that are focused, organized, and well developed.

2. Demonstrate increased self-confidence as a writer through interaction with peers and participation in collaborative groups.

3. Demonstrate an understanding of the paragraph in the context of the essay.

4. Write well-developed essays with attention to voice, audience, and purpose.

5. Demonstrate increased proficiency in the application of grammar and mechanics in the writing process.

6. Demonstrate an understanding of the research process by writing a paper that includes selection, evaluation, and use of appropriate documentation of sources.

BSA 025—INTRO TO COLLEGE WRITING II
Daily Schedule

Session #	Class Activity	Assignment for Next Session
#1	Orientation; Safety Rules; Pre-test	Read Chapter 1
#2	Chapter 1—The Writing Process; Video; Grammar Review	Complete Grammar Review
#3	Go Over Grammar Review; Computerized "Help" Lessons	Read Chapter 2
#4	Chapter 2—Generating Ideas; Essay of Introduction assigned	Write Essay of Introduction
#5	No Class Session (Word Processing Tutorial in LRC)	Complete Essay of Introduction Read Chapters 3 & 4
#6	**Essay of Introduction due;** Chapter 3—Process of Writing Chapter 4—Coherence	Read Chapter 5
#7	Chapter 5—Paragraph of Illustration; In-class writing	Read Chapter 6

Daily Schedule *(continued)*

#8	Chapter 6—Paragraph of Narration; In-class writing	Read Chapter 7
#9	Chapter 7—Paragraph of Description; In-class writing	Read Chapter 8
#10	Chapter 8—Process, In-class writing	Read Chapters 9 & 10
#11	Chapter 9—Definition; Chapter 10—Comparison & Contrast	Read Chapters 11 & 12
#12	Chapter 11—Classification; Chapter 12—Persuasion	Read Chapter 17
#13	Chapter 17—Writing an Essay; Persuasive Essay assigned	Select essay topic
#14	In-class work on essay topics (group work and brainstorming)	Write Persuasive Essay
#15	No Class Session	Complete Persuasive Essay Read Chapters 18 & 19
#16	**Persuasive Essay due;** Chapter 18—Types of Essays Chapter 19—Introduction, Conclusion, and Title	Read Chapter 13
#17	Chapter 13—Consistency and Parallelism; Informative Essay assigned	Write informative Essay
#18	In-class work on Essay (group work and brainstorming)	Continue writing/revision
#19	No Class Session	Complete Informative Essay Read Chapters 14 & 15
#20	**Informative Essay due;** Chapter 14—Sentence Variety; Chapter 15—Language Awareness	None
#21	Discussion of Research and Research Techniques; Research Paper assigned	Work on planning for research paper
#22	Notetaking discussion; Topic, thesis, planning due (group work and brainstorming)	None

Daily Schedule *(continued)*

#23	SIRS demonstration—LRC	Begin research process
#24	No Class Session—Library Source Search and Note-Taking	Continues Research process; begin note-taking
#25	Works Cited Page (bring sources to class); Parenthetical Reference discussion	Read Chapter 20 Continue note-taking
#26	Chapter 20—The Essay Question; Final discussion/questions on research paper	Write research paper
#27	No Class Session	Complete research paper
#28	**Research Papers due;** Discussion on Portfolio content and construction; Final in-class writing	Rewrite portfolio essays
#29	No Class Session	Complete rewriting and assemble portfolios
#30	**Portfolios due;** Research papers returned; ASSET post-assessment	None
#31	No Class Session	None
#32	No Class Session: Portfolios may be viewed in the instructor's office after	

_____
(time)   (date)

From June J. McManus, San Antonio College, TX

Assignment Sheet

Aug. 30   Intro: Course and TASP
Take up student information sheets. Five-minute journal entry on names.
Review Unit 6 in *Evergreen* before Pre-Test in Lab, Jan. 22.
Journal Instructions: *Evergreen*, pp. 12–15 and instruction sheet attached.

Sept. 1   In-class oral reading: "Three Types of Resistance to Oppression," Martin Luther King,
pp. 526–529 in *Evergreen*. Large group discussion. Journal response.

3   In-class paragraph. Turn in at end of period for evaluation.

6   Labor Day Holiday

8   Review for Pre-Test. (Bring Scantron #882 and #2 pencil Friday.)
Remember journal entry from *The Ranger* every Friday.

10   Lab Pre-Test. Come to class first.

13   Revision workshop in class

15   *Evergreen*, Unit 1, pp. 1–15.
In class practice of techniques.

17   Lab

20   *Evergreen*, Unit 2: The Paragraph
Read pp. 18–31, doing as many exercises as you can. Read sample paragraphs
carefully. Discuss paragraph #8, p. 40.

22   In-class paragraph

24   Lab

27   Usage lesson on paragraph #8. Revision workshop in class. Read Coherence,
Chapter 4, in Evergreen, pp. 42–65. Do some of each exercise.

29   Read outside of class in *Evergreen*, "A Life Defined by Losses and Delights," Nancy
Mairs, pp. 522–529. Look at coherence—order and transition.

Oct. 1   Lab

4   Review methods of development: illustration, narration, description, process,
definition, comparison and contrast, classification, persuasion in *Evergreen*,
pp. 68–161. (Look especially at first page of each discussion and sample paragraphs.)
Do some journal entries using these methods before Oct. 22, at least one by next class.
Draw for the method.

6   Read the paragraph you wrote (following the method you drew) aloud in class. Large
group competition with prizes.

8   Lab

11   Review journal requirements. Practice TASP handout. Read Unit 5 in *Evergreen*
"Writing the Essay," pp. 241–315, before class.

13   Write Practice TASP I.

15   Lab

| | 18 | Mid-Semester
Revision workshop in class for Practice TASP I. Discussion introductions and conclusions. Before class, read selection from *Hunger of Memory*, Richard Rodriguez, pp. 502–505. Do journal entry from #2 or #3 on p. 506 before class. |

        18   Mid-Semester
              Revision workshop in class for Practice TASP I. Discussion introductions and
              conclusions. Before class, read selection from *Hunger of Memory*, Richard Rodriguez,
              pp. 502–505. Do journal entry from #2 or #3 on p. 506 before class.

        20   Begin practice TASP II.

        22   Lab
              JOURNALS DUE (Include five paragraphs from Oct. 4, four *Ranger* entries, thirty
              entries total; circle ten dates of entries for me to read.)

        25   Finish TASP

        27   Revision workshop for Practice TASP II. Discuss development.

        29   Lab

Nov.   1   *Evergreen*, pp. 256–263, ordering and linking paragraphs. Look at your two practice
              TASPs in large groups.
              Honors Week

        3   Read before class "Beauty: When the Other Dancer is the Self," Alice Walker,
              pp. 480–486 in *Evergreen*.

        6   Lab
              Last day to drop (with Dean's approval only)

        8   Review essay techniques, audience, TASP writing prompts. Journal entry.

        10   Begin practice TASP III.

        12   Lab

        15   Finish practice TASP.

        17   Revision workshop for Practice TASP III.

        19   Lab

        22   Before class, read "How to Get the Most out of Yourself," pp. 499–502, in *Evergreen*.
              Look at writing assignments #2 and #3. In class journal entry. Discuss holistic
              grading.

        24   Begin practice TASP IV.

      25–26   Thanksgiving Holidays.

        29   Finish practice TASP.

Dec.   1   Large group discussion of Practice TASP IV. FINAL JOURNALS DUE (60 entries
              total. 30 new entries. Mark 10 for me to read of last 30.)

        3   Lab

        6   Review writing skills part of TASP

        8   Review for final exam

        10   Lab Post Test (Bring Scantron #882E & #2 pencil.)

Dec.   15   Final exam 11:00–1:30

From Patricia Malinowski, Finger Lakes Community College, NY

Course Syllabus,
GST 102—College Composition

Course Objectives

Overall Goal: To provide instruction and practice that will enable the student to write effectively in a variety of college and career situations and to develop requisite skills for entrance into English 101.

Objectives

1. To learn to identify major sentence parts.

2. To learn to combine sentences through coordination and subordination of ideas.

3. To learn to combine sentences into coherent, unified paragraphs.

4. To learn to identify and construct a variety of paragraphs using various patterns.

5. To build on the basic skills learned in paragraph writing in order to construct a well developed essay.

6. To acquire the habit of writing effectively.

7. To acquire the habit of editing all written work.

INTRODUCTION TO COMPOSITION

Tentative Calendar — Unit I

	9/8 Get Acquainted Orientation	9/10 Read *Evergreen* pp. 2–4 Journal #1 due
9/13 Read *Evergreen* pp. 5–13 Paragraph 1 due: (topic from Practice 3, p. 7 *or* Practice 5, p. 9)	9/15 Read *Evergreen* pp. 18–23	9/17 No class session Work on Journal #2 and Paragraph #2
9/20 Word processing Computer classroom	9/22 Read *Evergreen* pp. 23–29 Journal #2 due Paragraph #2 due, (topic to be assigned)	9/24 Read *Evergreen* pp. 29–38 Individual Chapter Test #1
9/27 Paragraph #3 due	9/29 Read *Evergreen* Chapter 7	10/1 Journal #3 due
10/4 Paragraph #4 due	10/6 Individual Chapter Test #2	10/8 No Class Session
10/11 Journal #4 due In-class Evaluation Paragraph		

INTRODUCTION TO COMPOSITION

Tentative Calendar — Unit II

10/11 Journal #4 due In-class Evaluation Paragraph	10/13 *Evergreen*, Chapter 19, pp. 291–296, Introductions and Conclusions; answer questions; do Writing Assignment 1, p. 294	10/15 Review Chapter 21 Chapter 21, re-test Mini-Essay #1 due, from topics on pp. 39–40
10/18 Journal #6 *Evergreen* Chapter 8, pp. 98–105; answer questions	10/20 Mini Essay #2 due, from topics, p. 107 Conferences Work on individual chapters	10/22 Journal #5 due Individual chapter tests Conferences
10/25 *Evergreen* Chapter 4, pp. 42–54; answer questions Do Writing Assignments 1, 2, 3	10/27 *Evergreen* Chapter 4, pp. 54–65; answer questions	10/29 Writing Assignments 4 & 5 Mini-Essay #3 due
11/1 Journal #8 due *Evergreen*, Chapter 5, pp. 68–76; answer questions	11/3 In-class writing	11/5 Mini-essay #4 due, topics p. 76
11/81 Journal #7 due Individual Chapter tests	11/9	11/11

INTRODUCTION TO COMPOSITION

Tentative Calendar — Unit III

11/15 Conferences	11/17 In-class Mini-essay	11/19 *Evergreen* Ch. 12; Read pp. 147–154, do Practices 1 & 2
11/22 *Evergreen* Ch. 12; Read pp. 156–159, read pp. 288–290	11/24 Thanksgiving Break No Class	11/26 Thanksgiving Break No Class
11/29 No Class Work on Essay #1, topics p. 159 or 290	12/1 Essay #1 due (Persuasive) In class: work on *Evergreen*, Ch. 17, pp. 245–256	12/3 *Evergreen*, Ch. 17, pp. 256–263, do Part D
12/6 Revision of Essay #1 due Read *Evergreen*, pp. 263–268	12/8 Essay #2 due, topic pp. 268–269 In class: Begin *Evergreen* Ch. 10, pp. 120–130	12/10 Review Highlights of *Evergreen*, Ch. 13
12/13 Revision of Essay #2 due Essay #3 due, topic from Practice 4, pp. 128–129 In class: Review Highlights of *Evergreen*, Ch. 14	12/15 Review and answer questions Essay #3 returned	12/17 In-class essay
12/20 Complete in-class essay	12/22 Conferences	

From Suzanne Doonan, Pennsylvania Institute of Technology, PA

Syllabus

Text

Evergreen with Readings, by Susan Fawcett and Alvin Sandberg
Available in the campus bookstore

Course Description

Writing organized paragraphs with correct grammar, punctuation, and spelling is the focus of this course.

Objectives

At the conclusion of the course, you will be able to:

> Write a paragraph with a good topic sentence and ideas that follow logically in the narrative, process, definition, compare/contrast, and classification forms.

> Edit your writing for errors in grammar, punctuation, and spelling.

Class Activities

We'll work together brainstorming, freewriting, writing drafts, revising, and editing your expository writing. Each week we'll focus on a list of commonly misspelled words and on the seven basic spelling rules of English words. We'll work through the grammar exercises to give you an intensive review of the rules of English grammar. Finally, we'll read essays from your text and discuss their writing strengths.

Each class will be important and unique. Please try to attend every class. If you can't attend, please find out from another student what you've missed, so that you'll be prepared for the next class.

Journal writing is an important skill-building activity. I encourage you to keep a journal in which you record your impressions, hopes, dreams, and challenges of your first semester at P.I.T. Daily writing will help you improve your writing skills, and contemplation of the changes you are making in your life will help you grow intellectually. The journals is your personal possession. It is not required, will not be collected, and will not count in any way toward your grade in this course. It will be a personal record of your success!

Good luck with your writing!

Course Outline

Week 1

Ch. 1 — Exploring the Writing Process, pp. 1–4
Ch. 2 — Generating Ideas, pp. 5–15
"A Brother's Murder" by Brent Staples, pp. 489–492

Week 2

Ch. 21 — The Simple Sentence, pp. 318–323
Ch. 29 — Prepositions, pp. 410–412

Week 3

Ch. 3 — The Process of Writing Paragraphs, pp. 18–41
"In Search of Bruce Lee's Grave" by Shanlon Wu, pp. 486–489

Week 4

Ch. 22 — Coordination and Subordination, pp. 324–339

Week 5

Ch. 4 — Achieving Coherence, pp. 42–65
"Hunger of Memory" by Richard Rodriguez, pp. 502–506

Week 6

Ch. 23 — Avoiding Sentence Errors, pp. 340–351
Ch. 6 — Narration, pp. 78–85
"One More Lesson" by Judith Cofer, pp. 492–496

Week 7

Ch. 24 — Present Tense (Agreement), pp. 352–362
"Beauty: When the Other Dancer is the Self," by Alice Walker, pp. 480–486

Week 8

Ch. 8 — Process, pp. 98–107
Ch. 27 — Nouns, pp. 387–393

Week 9

Ch. 28 — Pronouns, pp. 394–413
Ch. 11 — Classification, pp. 138–146
Ch. 25 — Past Tense, pp. 363–372
"How to Get the Most Out of Yourself" by Alan McGinnis, pp. 499–502

Week 10

Ch. 26 — The Past Participle, pp. 373–386
Ch. 9 – Definition, pp. 108–119
"A Life Defined by Losses and Delights" by Nancy Mairs, pp. 522–529

Week 11

Ch. 13 — Revising for Consistency and Parallelism, pp. 164–186
Ch. 10 — Comparison and Contrast, pp. 120–137
"Living with My VCR" by Nora Ephron, pp. 517–520

Week 12

Ch. 30 — Adjectives and Adverbs, pp. 414–421
Ch. 31 — The Apostrophe, pp. 422–427
Ch. 11 — Classification, pp. 138–146

Week 13

Ch. 14 — Revising for Sentence Variety, pp. 187–217
Ch. 32 — The Comma, pp. 428–437

Week 14

Ch. 15 — Revising for Language Awareness, pp. 218–234
Ch. 33 — Mechanics, pp. 438–447

Week 15

Ch. 17 — The Process of Writhing an Essay, pp. 242–271

Week 16

Final Exam

Spelling

Week 1—7

Ten words will be selected each week from the list of Commonly Misspelled Words on pages 458–459. In addition, we well review the spelling rules on pages 450–459.

Weeks 8–15

Each week, we will complete two to three of the practice exercises called "Look-Alikes/Sound-Alikes on pp. 461–473.

From Cliff Gardiner, Augusta College, GA

Course Description:
DEVELOPMENTAL WRITING II

Text: *Evergreen with Readings*

Typical Week-by-Week Progression Through the Text

Week 1:	Chapters 2 and 3
Week 2:	Chapter 17
Week 3:	Chapter 18, pp. 272–274; Chapter 19
Week 4:	Chapter 21; Chapter 22, pp. 324–331
Week 5:	Chapter 22, pp. 331–339; Chapter 23
Week 6:	Chapter 11 & Chapter 18, pp. 285–287; Chapter 13, pp. 164–179
Week 7:	Chapter 32
Weeks 8 and 9:	We do practice tests of grammar, mechanics, and usage in preparation for our state-mandated Collegiate Placement Examination (CPE), which students are required to pass in order to exit the course and go on to Freshman English.
Week 10:	Students write two 45-minute exam essays on topics sentenced by the instructor from a list distributed to students a week earlier; those who pass at least one essay proceed to phase two of the final exam, the CPE.

The "Laboratory" Component of the Course

Students are required to work independently on any aspect of writing they choose, for a total of two hours per week. I offer them several contexts for this individualized work; working in chapters from *Evergreen* that we won't be covering as an entire class (many choose this option), tutorial help in Augusta College's Writing Lab, or working in any of several supplementary texts and workbooks that we house in our library and our Learning Center.

Writing Assignments

Students write at least one essay per week. The first is done out of class, most of the others in class; students select one or two essays to revise out of class. They are encouraged to submit one of these essays to be considered for publication in *BrainPower*, a biannual magazine of developmental students' writing and artwork.

Students write primarily on assigned topics, although I always allow them a choice. We begin with (to use James Kinneavy's terms) expressive topics and progress to more referential topic.

English 100: Basic Writing
COURSE SYLLABUS

Content overview (subject to modification as warranted)

Week	Class Content	Homework Assignment(s)
1.	Diagnostic essay #1; introductory course overview	Appendix 2 Diagnostic essay #2
2.	Outlining principles; intro to eight parts of speech and the sentence	Chs. 21, 27, 29, 30
3.	Discovering the paragraph: brainstorming, selecting & narrowing topic sentence, ideas, writing, revising; coherence	Chs. 2, 3, 4 **Paper #1** (Ch. 6, Descr.)
4.	Process of subordination & coordination	Chs. 21–22
5.	Sentence errors: run-ons, splices, fragments; review of mechanics	Chs. 23, 30 **Paper #2** (Ch. 7, Narr.)
6.	**Review:** outlining, writing the paragraph, development, sentence sense	
☆ ☆ ☆ ☆ ☆	**Mid-Term Examination**	☆ ☆ ☆ ☆ ☆
7.	Editing process: proofreading methods, double-correction method, writing folder setup, revisions	Chs. 13, 14,15 Consistency, variety, language awareness
8.	The process paragraph	Ch. 8
9., 10.	Verbs (agreement): subject-verb agreement, troublesome verbs, separating verbs and subjects, agreement in questions and clauses	Chs. 24, 28 **Paper #3** (Process)
11.	Verb tenses (usage): present and past tense; the past participle	Chs. 24, 25, 26

☆ ☆ ☆ ☆ ☆	**Workshops: revisions, rewrites, CES work**	☆ ☆ ☆ ☆ ☆
12.	Improving the paragraph: overall cumulative review	Chs. 31, 32, 33
13.	The essay: mechanics (MLA), thesis, intro, title, conclusion; the four-paragraph essay	Chs. 17, 18F, 19
14.	The essay question: how to read, answer, and write a four- to five-paragraph essay answer (preparation for exit)	Ch. 20 **Paper #4** (Comp./contr. essay)
15.	General review: practice workshop for exit essay, objective final, and rewrites	
☆ ☆ ☆ ☆ ☆	**Final examination / collection of writing folders**	☆ ☆ ☆ ☆ ☆

Syllabus: ENO95

Week 1: Prewriting/Writing

<u>Monday, August 28</u>

In class:

- Introduction
- Complete Journal 1.

Homework:

- Purchase *Evergreen* text and large green envelope.
- Preview the textbook. What does it cover? How is it organized?
- Read Chapters 1 and 2. Do a focused freewrite on ONE topic in Practice 5, p. 9.
- Read Course Expectations and Syllabus.

<u>Wednesday, August 30</u>

In class:

- Hand in Practice 5, p. 9.
- Double check writing assignment.

Homework:

- Read chapter 3—pp. 18–26. Do IN BOOK, Practices 2 and 3.
- Review handout on Eight Parts of Speech.

<u>Friday, September 2</u>

In class:

- Discuss Topic Sentences.
- Computer: BEGIN and PETE. (Finish on own time. Save, but do not hand in.)

Homework:

- Finish Journal 2.
- ORGANIZE notebook into 7 sections: Syllabus, notes, grammar and grammar quizzes, research, journal, readings, formal paragraphs.
- Finish Chapter 3.
- Review Syllabus and Expectations for quiz.

Week 2: Vague/Specific

Monday, September 4

In class:

- Hand in Journal 2.
- Quiz on Syllabus and Course Expectations.
- Discuss Chapter 3—Support, Evidence.
- Activity: "Pictures."

Homework:

- Read pp. 218–223 on Vague Language.
- Read pp. 414–419 on Adjectives and Adverbs. Do Practice 5, p. 415 in book.
- Complete Planning Sheet for Paragraph 1.

Wednesday, September 6

In class:

- Discuss progress on Paragraph 1.
- Discuss Process of moving from Planning Stage to Writing.
- Computers: UNITY and VAGUE.

Homework:

- Begin rough draft, Paragraph 1.
- Finish UNITY, VAGUE. Save. Print. Proofread!
- Read pp. 317–323 on Subjects and Verbs.

Friday, September 8

In class:

- Hand in UNITY, VAGUE.
- Discuss Verbs—esp. Active Verbs.
- Computer: ACTIVE. Save. Switch seats. Revise. Save but don't print.

Homework:

- Finish Journal 3.
- Finish rough draft of Paragraph 1. Bring draft and object Monday!!
- *Actively* read "Disney's Perfect World," p. 277.

CLC: Chs. 2 and 26.

Week 3: Description

Monday, September 11

In class:

- Peer Review of Paragraph 1.
- Hand in Journal 3.
- Discuss Research 1.

Homework:
- Read "Disney." Quiz on Wednesday.
- FINISH FINAL DRAFT of Paragraph 1. Put drafts, peer review, and Planning Sheet in folder.
- Do Practice 2, p. 320 on subjects; Practice 8, p. 198, on compound verbs.
- Read Chapter 4—Coherence.

Wednesday, September 13

In class:
- QUIZ: "Disney's Perfect World."
- Create Title Page for Paragraph 1. Hand in Pragraph 1.
- Notes: Qualities of Descriptive Writing.
- Computer: TRANSIT. Due Monday.

Homework:
- Read Chapter 7—Descirption. Do Paragraphs 1 and 2 in book.
- Begin Planning Sheet Paragraph 2.
- Work on Research 1 and TRANSIT.

Friday, September 15

In class:
- Go over pp. 89–90.
- Work on Paragraph 2.

Homework:
- Finish Research 1 and TRANSIT.
- Finish Journal 4.
- Write rough draft of Paragraph 2.
- Read pp. 235–237. Notice revisions made.

CLC: Ch. 3: Subjects and Verbs.

Week 4: Revising on Computer

Monday, September 18

In class:
- Hand in Journal 4. Research 1, and TRANSIT.
- Discuss pp. 235–237—revisions.
- Computer: Begin putting Paragraph 2 on disk.
- Computer: Learn Spell Check [CTRL F4].

Homework:
- Finish rough draft on computer. Save. Print.
- *Actively* read "A Life Defined," pp. 522–525.
- Read Chapter 24 on Subject/Verb Agreement. Do exercises in book.

Wednesday, September 20

In class:

- Peer Review of Paragraph 2.
- Discuss Chapter 24.
- Computer: Revising Paragraph 2.

Homework:

- Finish Paragraph 2. Save. Run Spell Check. Proofread. Save. Print. Don't forget a Title Page. Make sure everything is in folder.
- Read Chapter 8 on Process Writing.
- Reread "A Life Defined."

Friday, September 22

In class:

- Hand in Paragraph 2 in folder.
- Notes: Process Writing—Chapter 8.
- Computer: GUM—practice with Chronological Order and Move command.

Homework:

- Finish Journal 5.
- Read Chapter 22: pp. 324–331. Do Practices 2 and 3.
- Review "A Life Defined."
- Read over Research 2 and 3.

CLC: Ch. 6: Subj./Verb Agreement.

Week 5: Process

Monday, September 25

In class:

- Hand in Journal 5.
- Form groups. Begin Research 2.
- LIBRARY VISIT.

Homework:

- Chapter 22: pp. 331–336. Do Practice 8.
- Complete Planning Sheet for Paragraph 3.
- Work on Research 2—due Friday.
- Read Process handout.

Wednesday, September 27

In class:

- QUIZ: "A Life Defined."
- Discuss Chapter 22.
- Discuss handout.
- Work on rough draft of Paragraph 3 and Research 2.

Homework:

- Finish rought draft. Make sure you have a topic sentence with a conjunctive adverb.
- Review Chapter 22. Finish Research 2.
- Actively read "Living with My VCR"—p. 517.

Friday, September 29

In class:

- Peer Review, Paragraph 3.
- Hand in Research 2.
- Discuss "VCR." (No quiz on this.)

Homework:

- Finish Journal 6.
- Finish Paragraph 3.
- Read Chapter 9—Definition.

CLC: Ch. 7: Sentence Types.

Week 6: Definition

Monday, October 2

In class:

- Hand in Journal 6.
- Hand in Paragraph 3.
- Notes: Definition.
- Final review of Chapter 22 quiz.
- Computer: CONNOT. Save. Proofread. Print. Hand in by Friday.

Homework:

- *Actively* read "How to Get the Most Out of Yourself"—pp. 499–502.
- Do Practice 5, pp. 110–111, TO HAND IN.
- Work on Research 3.

Wednesday, October 4

In class:

- Hand in Practice 5.
- Discuss "Yourself," and Practice 5, p. 110.
- QUIZ: Chapter 22.

Homework:

- Finish Research 3.
- Prepare for in-class paragraph—Definition.
- Finish CONNOT.

Friday, October 6

In class:

- Hand in Research 3 and CONNOT.
- In-class paragraph.

Homework:

- Read Chapter 5—Illustration. Do Practices 1 and 2 in book.
- Finish Journal 7.
- Read "Acting to Save Mother Earth," pp. 272–273.
- Read handout Definition and Illustration.

CLC: Test 1.

BREAK!!

Week 7: Examples

Monday, October 16

In class:

- Hand in Journal 7.
- Discuss Chapter 5, Examples, handout, and "Mother Earth," pp. 272–273.
- Revisit "How to Get the Most . . . Yourself," p. 499—looking for examples. Look at Building Blocks handout.
- Group work: Research 4.

Homework:

- Read pp. 237–239—revising, contd.
- Finish Research 4.
- Begin Planning Sheet for Paragraph 5.

Wednesday, October 18

In class:

- Library visit.
- Hand in Research 5.
- Finish Research 5 in library. Must be present—no makeups.

Homework:

- Read pp. 344–349 on Fragments.
- Finish planning, begin rough draft of Paragraph 5.
- Photocopy THREE articles on reserve in library to be ready for Research 6 on Monday.

Friday, October 20

In class:

- Discuss Fragments.
- Computer: DIAMOND—practice with fragments—from pp. 348–349.
- Work on Paragraph 5.

    Homework:

    - Finish DIAMOND. Proofread. Save. Print.
    - Finish Journal 8.
    - Finish rough draft of Paragraph 5.
    - Make sure you have photocopies of 3 articles.

CLC: CH 8: Fragments.

Week 8: Comparison/Contrast

Monday, October 23

In class:

- Hand in Journal 8.
- Peer Review: Paragraph 5.
- Research 6. Due at end of class.

    Homework:

    - Finish final draft of Paragraph 5.
    - Read handout on Comparison.
    - Read Chapter 10, pp. 120–128. Do Practices 1, 2, 3 in book.

Wednesday, October 25

In class:

- Hand in Paragraph 5.
- Discuss handout. Notes: Comparison and Contrast.
- Discuss Extra Credit Opportunity: Creating an essay from Paragraphs 4 and 5.
- Computer: Research 7.
- Computer: KELLOGG (from p. 343).

    Homework:

    - Finish Research 7.
    - Work on KELLOGG.
    - Read Chapter 17: pp. 242–248. Do Practice 1 in book.
    - Extra credit essay.

Friday, October 27

In class:

- Hand in Research 7.
- Role of Thesis Sentence. Chapter 17.
- Planning Essay 1—Comparison/Contrast.
- Go over Research 8. Class will use same article.

Homework:
- Finish Journal 9.
- Finish KELLOGG.
- Begin Research 8.
- Finish Planning Essay 1.

CLC: Ch. 9: Run-ons and Comma Splices.

Week 9: Comparison/Contrast, Research

<u>Monday, October 30</u>

In class:
- Hand in Journal 9. KELLOGG.
- Work on Essay 1 and Research 8.
- Computer: SCRABBLE (from p. 349).

Homework:
- Finish Research 8. Check this carefully!
- Read Chapter 17, pp. 263–271, on revising essays.
- Work on rough draft of Essay 1.
- Finish SCRABBLE.

<u>Wednesday, November 1</u>

In class:
- Hand in Research 8 and SCRABBLE.
- Discuss Note-Taking for Research. Start Research 9—green cards.
- Computer: COMPARE (from p. 283). Save. Discuss. Do not hand in.

Homework:
- Complete rough draft of Essay 1.
- Read Chapter 33, pp. 443–444, on quotations. Do in book Practice 4.
- Read articles carefully and take careful notes—some quotations and some paraphrases. Do this *meticulously!*

<u>Friday, November 3</u>

In class:
- Peer Review of Essay 1.
- Computer: RESEARCH 10—GIVING CREDIT.
- Work on final draft of Essay 1.

Homework:
- Finish Journal 10.
- Work on final draft of Essay 1.
- Work on Research 9 (notes) and Research 10 (on computer).
- Read: to be announced.

CLC: Chs. 12 and 14—Commas and Quotations Marks.

Week 10: Research

Monday, November 6

In class:

- Hand in Journal 10 and Research 9—NOTES.
- Begin Research 11—outlining or mapping Research essay.
- Work on final draft of Essay 1.

Homework:

- Finish final draft of Essay 1.
- Finish Research 10 and work on Research 11—outline.

Wednesday, November 8

In class:

- Hand in Essay 1 and Research 10.
- Work on Research 11. Arrange note-cards to follow outline.
- Read, discuss Model Research Essay.

Homework:

- Work on Research 11—outline.
- Work on writing Essay 2—Research from organized note-cards.

Friday, November 10

In class:

- In-class workshop on writing Essay 2.

Homework:

- Finish Journal 11.
- Finish Research 11.
- Read Chapter 28 on Pronoun Agreement.
- Read handout: Cause and Effect.

CLC: Test 2.

Week 11: Cause/Effect

Monday, November 13

In class:

- Hand in Journal 11 and Research 11— (outline).
- Discuss handout. Notes: Cause and Effect Analysis.
- Discuss Chapter 28: Pronouns and Agreement.
- Computer: Getting Research Essay on disk.

Homework:

- Reread pp. 243–244—"Making a Difference."
- Read handout on racism.
- Continue writing rough draft of Essay 2.

Wednesday, November 15

In class:

- Discuss pp. 243–244.
- Discuss racism handout.
- Read "Disney" handout. Discuss possible effects.
- Introduction: Fallacies—errors in cause and effect.

Homework:

- Read Practice 10, p. 408. Make corrections.
- Read Chapter 31, pp. 422–425, on apostrophes.

Friday, November 17

In class:

- QUIZ: on computer—PEARL.
- Computer: Finish rough draft of Essay 2.

Homework:

- Finish Journal 12.
- Read over rough draft. CHECK all quotes and paraphrases against your note-cards! Then check against articles themselves!

CLC: Ch. 10—Pronouns.

Week 12: Cause/Effect; Persuasion

Monday, November 27

In class:

- Hand in Journal 12.
- Discuss Chapter 31—Apostrophes.
- Peer Review of Essay 2.

Homework:

- Revise Essay 2.
- Read over Appendix 2, homonyms—pp. 461–472.

Wednesday, November 29

In class:

- Discuss homonyms.
- Computer: Final work on Essay 2.

Homework:

- Proofread Essay 2. Get everything ready to put in green envelope.
- Read "Zora Neale Hurston," pp. 472–473.

Friday, December 1

In class:

- ESSAY 2 DUE.
- Computer: Hurston (from pp. 472–473).

Homework:

- Finish Journal 13.
- Read Chapter 12, Persuasion. Do Practices 1 and 2.

CLC: Chs. 13 and 15: Apostrophes and Homonyms

Week 13: Persuasion

Monday, December 4

In class:

- Hand in Journal 13.
- Discuss Chapter 12. Use Building Blocks handout.
- Notes: Persuasion.
- Discuss summary writing.

Homework:

- Read pp. 175–178 Parallelism. Do Practice 10—1–5—in book.
- Read "Some Thoughts About Abortion," p. 510.

Wednesday, December 6

In class:

- Discuss Quindlen essay.
- Go over Research 12.
- Begin planning Essay 3—EXIT Essay.

Homework:

- Complete Planning Sheet for Essay 3.
- Work on Research 12.
- Read pp. 224–225 on wordiness.

Friday, December 8

In class:

- Group work—discussing Planning Sheets.
- Computer: WORDY.

Homework:

- Finish Journal 14. Hand in Writing Strengths and Weaknesses with it.
- Write rough draft of Essay 3.
- Finish Research 12.

CLC: Chs 20, 21, 22: Modifiers and Parallelism.

Week 14:

Monday, December 11

In class:

- Hand in Journal 14 and Writing Strengths and Weaknesses.
- Hand in Research 12.
- Workshop on final essay.

Homework:

- Finish rough draft of Essay 3.

Wednesday, December 13

In class:

- Peer Review of Exit Essay (#3).
- Workshop on final draft.
- Computer: ERRORS—proofreading.

Homework:

- Finish final draft of Essay 3.

Friday, December 15

In class:

- Hand in Essay 3.

Good luck next semester!

English 109, Basic Writing Skills II

Step 1:   I administer the Diagnostic Test accompanying the text that covers grammar, usage, and mechanics skills. Based on student results, I recommend intensive Learning Lab work, including individual tutoring, group sessions, and independent work materials (computer programs, video and audio materials).

I administer a mid-term skills assessment and a final mastery test. A passing grade is 70% or better.

Step 2:   I introduce the students to Microsoft Word on our Macintosh computers and assign the paragraphs on pages 38–40. For this assignment and all that follow, I ask students to submit their choice of a prewriting exercise, rough draft, and final copy.

Step 3:   Class time consists of discussion of readings (one each week), chapters that fit our needs (this varies, depending on the types of errors I am spotting in papers), discussion of rhetoric (the first half of our 15-week course concentrates on paragraph writing, the second half on short essays). My students generate many papers, creating a writing portfolio for themselves. I collect their folders for "official grading" three times during the semester, reading all papers and grading the ones they have chosen as "best."

Step 4:   A student's final grade is a synthesis of all the areas covered in class, plus level of participation and attendance. Lots of independent textbook reading is required in my class. I encourage students to check any pages we haven't covered in class against my text or with the tutor. I have a very close relationship with the Learning Lab and believe that students need to view their work from as many perspectives as possible. Probably half the time spent on our class is spent at the Lab.

From William Thomas, Los Angeles Trade Technical College, CA

Los Angeles Trade Technical College

Course Overview

English 28 introduces students to the principles and techniques of essay writing and reviews the well-constructed paragraph. Practice includes the writing of descriptive, narrative, expository, and argumentative essays of one or more paragraphs. Credit for the course meets the skills required for an Associate in Arts degree. Students also receive preparation to enter English 101, which is required for transfer to a four-year college or university. The prerequisite for this course is English 21 or equivalent ability. In a workshop atmosphere with study teams, you will work collaboratively with other students, participating in English form, grammatical and punctuation exercises, and critiquing one another's papers. You will write weekly papers, both in class and at home, and complete a number of proficiency inventories. You will explore cross-cultural issues and prepare a brief report on a selected aspect of a culture other than your own. You will read, note answers, and thoughtfully critique readings in the textbook.

Text: Fawcett & Sandberg, *Evergreen with Readings*, Fifth Edition; dictionary & thesaurus

Course Schedule

Class Meetings: MWF — 8:00 a.m. — F240

Each week is organized into class activity including homework, writing review and reading critiques, and writing homework assignment for the following week.

Weekly Assignments (Note: Reading and practice exercises should be completed by the Monday of the week they are to be reviewed. Do not complete practices that require writing a paragraph or essay, unless so directed by your instructor. Please complete all short-answer practices. The first draft of the homework paper is due on the following Monday, a second draft should be prepared by Wednesday, and a final draft is due on Friday. Late papers will result in lower grades.)

Aug. 21   Activity: Orientation to class. Homework: Autobiography—What Makes You Tick?

Aug. 28   Activity: Select best autobiography. "Getting Started" (pp. 1–15) and "The Simple Sentence" (pp. 318–323), and writing resumes and cover letters. Homework: Write a resume and a cover letter.

Sept. 4
Activities: Computer lab, and "Discovering the Paragraph" (pp. 17–41). Reading: Walker "Beauty: When the Other Dancer Is the Self" (pp. 480–486). Homework: "Description." Your choice (pp. 38–41).

Sept. 11
Activities: Computer lab, "The Process of Writing an Essay" (pp. 242–250), "Achieving Coherence" (pp. 42–65), and "Coordination and Subordination" (pp. 324–339).

Sept. 18
Activities: "The Process of Writing an Essay" (pp. 251–271), "Illustration" (pp. 68–76), and "Avoiding Sentence Errors" (pp. 340–351). Reading: Staples "A Brother's Murder" (pp. 489–492). Homework: "Illustration" (p. 76).

Sept. 25
Activities: "Types of Essays" (pp. 272–290), "Narration" (pp. 78–85), and "Present Tense" (pp. 352–362). Reading: Cofer "One More Lesson" pp. 492–496. Homework: "Narration" (p. 85).

Oct. 2
Activities: "The Introduction, the Conclusion, and the Title" (pp. 219–299), "Description" (pp. 86–96), and "Past Tense" (pp. 363–372). Reading: McGinnis "How to Get the Most Out of Yourself" (pp. 499–502).

Oct. 9
Activities: "Revising for Sentence Variety" (pp. 187–217), "Process" (pp. 98–107), and "The Past Participle" (pp. 373–386). Reading: Rodriguez "Hunger of Memory" (pp. 502–506). Homework: "Process" (p. 107).

Oct. 16
Activities: "The Essay Question and the Summary (pp. 301–315), "Definition" (pp. 108–119) and "Nouns" (pp. 387–393). Homework: "Definition" (p. 119).

Oct. 23
Activities: "Revising for Language Awareness" (pp. 218–234), and "Comparison and Contrast" (pp. 120–136), and "Pronouns" (pp. 394–409). Homework: "Compare/Contrast" (p. 137).

Oct. 30
Activities: "Putting Your Revision Skills to Work" (pp. 235–240), "Classification" (pp. 138–145), and "Prepositions" (pp. 410–413). Reading: Quindlen "Some Thoughts About Abortion" (pp. 510–513). Homework: "Classification" (p. 146).

Nov. 6
Activities: "Persuasion" (pp. 147–160) and "Adjectives and Adverbs" (pp. 414–421). Reading: Klagsbrun "On Kids and Couples" (pp. 513–517). Homework: "Persuasion" (pp. 160–161).

Nov. 13
Activities: "Revising for Consistency and Parallelism" (pp. 164–186) and "The Comma" (pp. 428–439). Homework:

Nov. 20
Activities: "Mechanics" (pp. 438–447). Reading: Ephron "Living with My VCR" (pp. 517–520). Homework: Essay on a new type of technology (p. 520).

Nov. 27
Activities: Cross-cultural panels. Discussion of research techniques. Reading: Mairs "A Life Defined by Losses and Delights" (pp. 522–525). Homework: Selection and outline of cross-cultural essay.

Dec. 4
Activities: Student reports on research. Reading: King "Three Types of Resistance to Oppression" (pp. 526–529). Homework: Cross-cultural essay.

Dec. 11
Activities: Review of Class. No homework assignment.

The final examination will be held between December 13 and 21.

From Ann Richey, Interboro Institute, NY

Weekly Schedule

Evergreen = E   *Interactions* = I

Exercises in E will be assigned on a weekly basis, some as in-class work and others as homework.

Week 1	Introductions, Business I, p. 528 "The Man in the Water" Reading Handouts E, Ch. 17 The Process of Writing an Essay
Week 2	E, Ch. 5 & 18A Illustration E, Ch. 2 Generating Ideas E, Ch. 19A The Introduction
Week 3	E, Chs. 12 and 18H Persuasion I, p. 471 "Electronic Gizmos Make Us Stupid" I, p. 475 "The Beep Goes On" E, Ch. 19 B & C The Conclusion & The Title E, Ch. 22 Coordination and Subordination **ESSAY #1 DUE: Illustration**
Week 4	Persuasion, cont. I, p. 458 "Television Addiction"/Reading Handout I, p. 461 "Why I Quit Watching Television" I, p. 450 "Taking a Byte Out of Privacy" "Coordination and subordination" extra practice **ESSAY #2 DUE: Persuasion**
Week 5	Research Paper Library Tools Using research material Endnotes & Bibliography
Week 6	E, Ch. 6 & 18B Narration E, Ch. 32 B, C, D The Comma E, p. 489 "A Brother's Murder"
Week 7	In-class workshop on research paper E, Ch. 26 The Past Participle **ESSAY #3 DUE: Narration**

Week 8	Review for Mid-term Exam
	Mid-term Exam (2 parts: Essay and Mechanics)

Week 9   E, Chs. 10 & 18F Comparison/Contrast
I, p. 264 "Love Is Never Enough"
E, Ch. 21 The Simple Sentence (identifying subjects and verbs)
E, Ch. 24 Present Tense/Agreement
ESSAY #4 DUE: Comparison/Contrast (in-class essay)

Print and Electronic Resources
for Instructors of Developing Writers

Print

Periodicals

College Composition and Communication. Urbana, IL: NCTE/CCCC. Quarterly, beginning 1950. Subscriptions: 1111 Kenyon Road, Urbana, IL 61801.

College English. Urbana, IL: NCTE College Section. Eight times a year, beginning 1939. Subscriptions: 1111 Kenyon Road, Urbana, IL 61801.

Journal of Basic Writing. New York: City University of New York Instructional Resource Center. Twice a year, beginning 1978. Subscriptions and submissions: Instructional Resource Center, City University of New York, 535 East 80th Street, New York, NY 10021.

Research in the Teaching of English. Athens: University of Georgia, NCTE Committee on Research. Three times a year, beginning 1967. Subscriptions: 1111 Kenyon Road, Urbana, IL 61801.

Teaching English in the Two-Year College. Urbana, IL: NCTE. Quarterly, beginning 1974. Subscriptions: 1111 Kenyon Road, Urbana, IL 61801.

The Writing Instructor. Los Angeles: University of Southern California. Quarterly, beginning 1981. Subscriptions and submissions: 817 W. 34th Street, Fourth Floor, University of Southern California, Los Angeles, CA 90089.

General Bibliographies

Enos, Theresa, ed. *Sourcebook for Basic Writing Teachers.* New York: Random House, 1987.

Lindemann, Erika. *Longman Bibliography of Composition and Rhetoric: 1984–1985 and 1986.* New York: Longman, 1987, 1988.

Tate, Gary, ed. *Teaching Composition: Twelve Bibliographic Essays.* Fort Worth: Texas Christian University Press, 1987.

Electronic Resources

gopher://info.asu.edu/11/asu-cwis/education/other (Education gophers)
gopher://info.asu.edu/11/asu-cwis/education/journal (Education journals and newsletters)
http://english-server.hss.cmu.edu/langs.html (Language and Linguistics)
http://www.fwl.org (Far West Laboratory)
http://www.olemiss.edu/depts.project_leap (Project Leap)

http://teams.lacoe.edu (Teams Distance Learning)

http://www.biddeford.com/learningpath (The Learning Path)

http://erc-web.te.columbia.edu (Urban Education Web)

http://199.20.120.suwp.htm (The Sanford Writing Project)

http://english-server.hss.cmu.edu (The English Server)

listserv@uhccv.muhcc.hawaii.edu (Teaching in the Community College)

listserv@listserv.Arizona.EDU (Open Forum for Learning Assistance
Professionals)

http://www.ed.gov/pubs/ResearachrsGuide/Services.html (U.S. Dept of
Education)

http://www.mala.bc.ca/www/wac/wac.htm (Writing Across the Curriculum)

THE HOUGHTON MIFFLIN COMMUNITY OF WRITERS
SCHOLARSHIP PROGRAM

Every community is established with a view to some good. —Plato

As a leader in developmental education, Houghton Mifflin is proud to offer your students the opportunity to share their writing with others and earn valuable scholarships.

Scholarships

Three scholarships—$500 first prize, $300 second prize, $200 third prize—will be awarded toward tuition reimbursement. The winners will be chosen by a panel of judges comprised of instructors teaching courses in developmental writing. Scholarship recipients will be announced by October 1, 1996. All participants will be recognized with a certificate of appreciation.

Who Is Eligible?

Every institution of post-secondary education in the United States and Canada offering a developmental writing course, *regardless of which textbook is used,* is welcome to nominate **one** student for the scholarship.

Entry forms are available from your Houghton Mifflin representative or can be obtained by calling the Houghton Mifflin Faculty Services Center at 1-800-733-1717.

How Do You Apply?

1) Please have your students write essays on this topic:

    What Is a Community?

    Students should be encouraged to interpret the topic as broadly as possible.

2) Essays should not exceed 750 words.

3) Then, please submit the essay you deem **best** along with a completed entry form, to

    Pamela Laskey
    Houghton Mifflin Company, College Division
    222 Berkeley Street
    Boston, MA 02116

4) All entries must be postmarked by July 15, 1996.

Submissions Wanted from Students and Instructors

From Students: As students are essential members of the Evergreen Community, we invite them to send us their comments on any aspect of writing, writing classes, or English classes in general—what they like or dislike, what works best, what just doesn't ever seem to work, what their life goals are, and how they think writing and English will help them achieve those goals. In sum, we are open to receiving just about anything students want to say that is related to *Evergreen,* writing, or the study of English. We will publish a portion of the student submissions in the next edition of *The Evergreen Community.*

From Instructors: Please send us your teaching ideas, reading lists, course outlines, or syllabi for possible inclusion in the Second Edition of *The Evergreen Community.* We want to keep the Community growing, and making this collection as interesting and useful as possible is an important part of making that happen.

Options for Getting Your Submissions to Us

FAX: Please include a copy of your completed submission form with your submission and fax them to us at 617.351.1134

Internet: We welcome e-mail submissions. To send us your submission using this option, please provide—in your own format—all of the relevant information that we ask for on the submission form and send your submission to the following address:

Ellen_Darion@hmco.com

Thank you !!!!

The Evergreen Community Submission Form

Please complete and enclose this form with your *Evergreen Community* submission.

Instructors and Students:

Name _____

School _____

Address _____

_____

Phone _____ Fax _____

Internet _____

Instructors Only:

Course(s) in which you have used *Evergreen* or *Evergreen with Readings* (please specify which version)

_____

_____

_____